Everything Has Two Handles

The Stoic's Guide to the Art of Living

Ronald Pies

HAMILTON BOOKS

A member of
THE ROWMAN & LITTLEFIELD PUBLISHING GROUP
Lanham • Boulder • New York • Toronto • Plymouth, UK

Library of Congress Control Number: 2007940211
ISBN-13: 978-0-7618-3951-4 (paperback : alk. paper)
ISBN-10: 0-7618-3951-8 (paperback : alk. paper)

This book is dedicated to the memory of my mother, Frances Pies Oliver,
who understood the "rational essence" of the Stoic world view
and gently transmitted it to her children.

"Everything has two handles: one by which it may be borne, another by which it cannot."

—Epictetus

Contents

Acknowledgments

I wish to thank Ira Allen and Linda Orlando for their expert assistance in editing this book. I also wish to thank Richard Berlin MD for his reading of the manuscript; Cynthia Geppert MD for her professional and spiritual inspiration; and Robert Deluty PhD for his encouragement during the early development of the manuscript. Finally, I thank my wife, Nancy Butters LICSW, for her patience and support.

Introduction

This is not a book for philosophers, nor is it a work of great scholarship. It is simply a book dedicated to the intelligent layperson who wants to live well and happily. While the principles discussed here are ancient, I believe they are as relevant to *our* lives—here and now—as they were to the Greek and Roman philosophers who first developed them. And since, in some respects, our modern lives present even more challenges and stresses than the ancient Stoic philosophers knew, the lessons of these sages may be even more relevant today than they were two millennia ago.

My aim is to let the ideas of Stoicism "bubble up" to the surface of our understanding, rather than to present them as a series of lecture topics. I hope you will find that, as each of the philosophical passages is presented, you will begin to understand both what Stoicism is and how it can make an important difference in your life. Although I will focus on one of the later Stoic philosophers—the great Roman Emperor, Marcus Aurelius (121-180 C.E.)—I will also draw upon other ancient and modern sources when it serves our purposes, including many from the Judaic and Christian traditions.

One of the misconceptions about Stoicism is that it lacks a spiritual basis—that it's just "cold, hard logic." In reality, Stoic philosophy draws on deep spiritual roots, and many people of faith will find parallels with their own religious background. (Those familiar with Buddhist and Taoist philosophies will find many features in common with Stoic philosophy.) In addition to citing some of these religious and spiritual sources, I will be brash enough to offer some commentary of my own, as well as some composite case vignettes, based on my own experience as a psychiatrist. (All names are fictitious, and most of the characters in the case vignettes represent several actual or typical patients.) Occasionally, I'll even throw in a joke or two, since the Stoics were not renowned for their rollicking sense of humor—and keeping your sense of humor is one of the keys to health and happiness!

Before plunging into Stoic philosophy, a little orientation may be useful. When you hear the word "stoic," what comes to mind? Maybe a character from Masterpiece Theater? One of those "stiff-upper-lip" 19th-century-British types, who keep their emotions under such tight wraps that their faces seem to be stitched in place? Or, if you are a "baby boomer" who grew up with the TV show, "Star Trek"—one of my favorites—maybe the character of the Vulcan, Mr. Spock, comes to mind. It turns out that Mr. Spock does share some features with the ancient Stoic philosophers, although perhaps not others. (For one thing, Mr. Spock is sometimes more focused on *mastering* his emotions than on *embracing a view of the world* that ultimately makes such "mastery" unnecessary.)

To be sure, "stoicism" has acquired something of a bad reputation. For many of us raised in the 60s—with its "let it all hang out" credo—the idea of being "stoical" sounds a lot like being, well, uptight and stuffy. Ours has been an age in which *expressing* emotion has been valued much more highly than *understanding* emotion—or realizing how our emotional over-reactions can detract from our happiness. The pioneers of cognitive-behavioral therapy (CBT), such as Dr. Albert Ellis and Dr. Aaron Beck, have long recognized this. Ellis, in particular, draws heavily on the Stoics (especially the slave, Epictetus) in formulating what he calls "Rational Emotive Behavioral Therapy" (REBT).

I hope to show you that genuine Stoicism is much more than keeping a stiff upper lip or tamping down your feelings with an iron rod. Stoicism, on the contrary, is a kind of mental and spiritual outlook. Indeed, depending on how we understand Stoic concepts like "logos," we could say that the Stoic is *someone who aims to live in accordance with God's, or Nature's, eternal laws.* Although you will find many passages by various Stoic writers to support the idea of emotional *modulation*, the Stoic ideal was not an emotionless, unfeeling human being. Rather, there is a "moderate middle ground" that best suits us as rational creatures. As Marcus Aurelius tells us, "Perfection of character possesses this: to live each day is if the last, to be neither feverish nor apathetic, and not to act a part" (Farquharson, 52). Indeed, the Stoics are said to strive for *apatheia,* but it would be a mistake to translate this as "apathy" in a negative sense; rather, *apatheia* implies a kind of *equanimity of spirit.* Marcus tells us, "A man's joy is to do what is proper to man, and man's proper work is kindness to his fellow man . . ." (Farquharson, 56, emphasis mine). So Marcus is far from wishing that we suppress all forms of joy! His aim is to teach us to find true joy through benevolent action, in accordance with our natural reason. We find a similar sentiment expressed by the Jewish sage, Rav

Eliyahu of Vilna, known as the Vilna Gaon (1720–97). He tells us, "Desires must be purified and idealized, not exterminated" (Baron, 1985).

The Stoic aims to understand "the way things are," and to live accordingly. And, although you do not have to believe in God to be a Stoic, you do need to understand how the universe is, well, *set up*. When we understand and accept the way things are, we find ourselves at peace, and are free to pursue our higher pleasures. When we refuse to accept the way things are, we make ourselves (and often others) unhappy. When you live your life according to Stoic principles, you don't need to tamp down your feelings—rather, the feelings you have are actually *appropriate* to "the way things are."

By now, you may already be thinking, "But aren't there times when we should *not* accept the way things are? When there are terrible social injustices, for example, aren't we obligated to *change* the status quo?" Those are excellent questions—and ones which, in my view, the Stoics answer with a very clear and forceful "*Yes!*" To understand this, we must understand that a part of "the way things are" is our own set of values and aspirations. Our intention to make the world a better place is no less a part of reality than rocks, trees, or turtles—and is certainly no less real than the social evils we seek to overturn. Thus, we have every right—and even a responsibility—to try to change things for the better. But when we have exerted every effort in doing so, and failed, we are not under any additional obligation to make ourselves miserable!

And so, Stoicism has a lot in common with that admittedly clichéd statement often posted at 12-step meetings: "God, grant me the serenity to accept the things I cannot change, the courage to change the things I can, and the wisdom to know the difference." Stoicism is not passive acceptance of the status quo, but a reasoned understanding of the way things are, and a rational determination to better what can be bettered—including ourselves.

That said, even the sages can lose their way. Sometimes, for example, the Stoic philosophers go a bit farther than I'm prepared to follow in urging us to restrain our emotions. This sometimes comes out in their views of the grieving process, or even of overwhelming joy. We needn't feel obligated to follow the Stoics slavishly in their approach to such emotional states. Rather, as philosopher A.C. Grayling reminds us—and as behavioral neurologists have recently affirmed—"Reason and feeling are equally great gifts, and equally necessary. If either is untempered by the other, the result can only be spiritual and intellectual impoverishment"(2002, 5). The same idea was argued more forcefully still by Dr. Samuel Johnson:

> Many . . . teach us not to trust ourselves with favorite enjoyments, not to indulge the luxury of fondness, but to keep our minds always suspended in such

indifference that we may change the objects about us without emotion. . . . An attempt to preserve life in a state of neutrality and indifference is unreasonable and vain. (Johnson, 1750)

Alright—enough prologue. Let us hear from the Masters, and see how their wisdom might apply to our own quest for a better life.

Note: Unless otherwise specified, quotations from Marcus Aurelius are taken from George Long's 1910 translation of *The Meditations*. That work, and all other sources used at length, is in the public domain. The one exception to this is Robin Campbell's 1969 translation of Seneca's *Letters*. For their kind permission to use this material, I am beholden to Penguin Classics (U.K.).

Chapter One

Thinking and Feeling

Things do not touch the soul, for they are external and remain immovable; but our perturbations come only from the opinion which is within. . . . The universe is transformation, life is opinion.

—Marcus Aurelius (Long, 54)

"Things do not touch the soul." This deceptively simple statement is the keystone in the arch of Stoic philosophy. Consider the case of Angela, a 28-year old divorced mother of two, struggling to "be a good wife and mother." When her five-year old daughter, Tiffany, began "acting up" in school, as well as having temper tantrums at home, Angela went into a depressive tailspin. She began to spend more and more time in bed, gave up a lot of her usual activities, and started to doubt her own value as a mother and a human being. "Tiffany is making me nuts!" Angela told her therapist. "She keeps yelling at me, no matter what I do, and always tells me what a bad mother I am. When I talked to one of my girlfriends about it, all she did was rag on me about how I need to 'discipline' Tiffany, as if I haven't tried! That *really* got me upset! I guess maybe I am a bad mother, if my daughter and my girlfriend think I'm such a screw-up."

Any of us—but especially mothers of young children—will sympathize with Angela. In fact, you might be saying, "Hey, yeah—I'd be depressed, too, if those things were happening to me." Maybe so. But the curious thing is that *not every mother would become clinically depressed, given exactly the same set of unfortunate circumstances.* Unhappy, yes—but severely depressed, no. Why is that? The Stoic answer is very similar to that of modern-day cognitive-behavioral therapists: Angela is depressed not because Tiffany is making her "nuts," or because her girlfriend was insensitive—but because of the way Angela is *thinking*.[1] Angela is tormenting herself with a number of self-defeating and irrational ideas, such as, "If my daughter yells at me, that must mean I'm a

1

bad mother," and, "If my girlfriend criticizes me, that means I have to become upset about it."

In Stoic terms, it is Angela's opinion about these external events—not the events themselves—that are making her upset. Change your opinions, change the way you feel!

Of course, this is often easier said than done, and even a Stoic is bound to say "Ouch!" if someone steps hard on his toe. We are not in complete control of how we feel—but we have much more influence over our emotions than we are led to believe by pop music, movies, and our "victim-oriented" culture.

But what is Marcus's point about the universe and "transformation"? I think this will become clear as we proceed. But for now, the next time you are upset over some fairly trivial event, ask yourself the following questions: "How important will this problem be to me or anybody else, a thousand years from now? Or a year from now? Or even a week from now?" Most of the time, your answer is likely to be, "Not terribly important." The universe is all about change, and your opinion about such change governs the way you feel. As Shakespeare put it in Hamlet (II.ii.253), "There is nothing either good or bad but thinking makes it so."

∽

We are what we think. All that we are arises with our thoughts. With our thoughts we make the world. Speak or act with a pure mind, and happiness will follow you as your shadow, unshakable. . . . Your worst enemy cannot harm you as much as your own thoughts, unguarded. But once mastered, no one can help you as much, not even your father or your mother.
— *From the* Dhammapada, *Trans. Thomas Byrom (in Kornfield 1993, 5)*

∽

Begin the morning by saying to yourself, I shall meet with the busybody, the ungrateful, arrogant, deceitful, envious, unsocial. All these things happen to them by reason of their ignorance of what is good and evil . . . [but] I can neither be injured by any of them . . . nor can I be angry with my kinsman, nor hate him.
—Marcus Aurelius (Long, 19)

∽

Whatever man you meet, say to yourself at once: 'What are the principles this man entertains about human goods and ills?' . . . then it will not seem surprising or strange . . . if he acts in certain ways . . .
—Marcus Aurelius (Farquharson 1946, 54–5)

Jim was a basket case by the time he arrived at work each morning. With a 45-minute commute into Boston, he invariably found himself fuming at "the morons out there who don't know how to drive." Once, when someone cut Jim off on the highway, Jim pulled up about ten feet behind the driver—at 60 miles per hour—and, as he put it, "just lay on the horn for ten minutes, all the way into Boston." But Jim's problems weren't just on the road. When he'd arrive at work, only to find all the parking spaces taken, Jim's blood would boil. Once, when someone quickly pulled into a space just ahead of him, Jim started honking the horn, swearing at the person, and nearly came to blows.

How do you think Jim might have reacted if he had engaged himself in the following "internal dialogue"?

"OK, it's a pain in the butt that this guy just grabbed a parking space right before I did. That was rude. But, I suppose he's running late, too, and he's just as anxious as I am to get into the office. Maybe he wasn't raised to have good manners, or maybe he just didn't see me trying for the same space. Anyway, as Tony Soprano says, 'Whaddya gonna do?' There are millions of impolite and thoughtless people out there, and I'll probably meet up with two or three more of them before the day's over! I guess life will go on."

Marcus makes the further point that such thoughtless boors *do not have it in their power to injure us* by reason of their thoughtlessness, nor need we end up "hating" such individuals. In fact, the originator of Rational Emotive Behavioral Therapy (REBT), Dr. Albert Ellis, would remind us that even labeling someone a "thoughtless boor" is overreacting. True, some people often exhibit thoughtless or boorish behavior, but that doesn't brand them as a "boor" now and forevermore. Indeed, when we try to understand how some annoying people come to be the way they are—learning "the principles this man entertains about human goods and ills"—we sometimes feel a bit less angry and dismissive toward the person. We may learn, for example, that the guy who pulled into the space ahead of Jim came from a family in which all the kids were taught to "Look out for Number One" above all else.

This may seem like a "touchy-feely" response to evil-doers, but Ellis's point actually reflects a profound ethical and religious principle: namely, that a person is more than the sum or his or her bad actions. Each of us has intrinsic worth simply by virtue of our common humanity, and someone who exhibits boorish behavior today may change tomorrow. In the Judaic tradition, we find this idea expressed in the *Talmud*, as follows: "Do not despise any person . . . for there is no person who does not have an hour and no thing that does not have its place" (Pirke Avot 4:3). Rabbi Shlomo Toperoff adds, "If you despise any man, you despise God . . . do not, therefore, despise the whole person even if you should discover an objectionable trait in his character. Be patient and you may yet discover that he possesses an admirable quality" (Toperoff, 203). In the Christian tradition, we find this wonderfully humane sentiment expressed by Thomas a Kempis in the essay "On Bearing with the Faults of Others": "There is no man without his faults, none without his burden. None is sufficient in himself; none is wise in himself; therefore, we must support one another, comfort, help, teach, and advise one another" (*Counsels on the Spritual Life* 1995, 40–1).

I know—it's hard to feel so "supportive" when somebody has just darted ahead of you into that last parking space! But if you start thinking differently about such behavior today, it will become easier to stay calm in the future.

∿

Rabbi Joseph Gelberman PhD is considered one of the foremost masters of Kabbala, that famous collection of Jewish mystical writings. He is also a psychotherapist—and has some very down-to-earth things to teach us about emotions:

> *Of all the tyrants in the world, our own attitudes are the fiercest warlords—the tyranny of the self over the self. Anger is a tyranny that you have established in your own heart and mind. . . . All anger really does is steal your freedom. Instead, accept the adversity you may be experiencing, reject anger and defeat, and let those harmful emotions go. (2000, 54)*
>
> *Fear is only a tyrant that is empowered by permission. We are the ones who open the door and let it slip in. (49)*

∿

> Get rid of the judgment, you are rid of the 'I am hurt'; get rid of the 'I am hurt,' you are rid of the hurt itself.
> —Marcus Aurelius (Farquharson 1946, 19)

Linda had been looking forward to the wedding of her college roommate, Jen, for months, and fully expected to be among the bridesmaids. But when the wedding announcement arrived, it was just a "generic" card, with no personal message at all. Linda was crushed. She began to re-play all the conversations she and Jen had had over the past year, and to inspect all their email exchanges for any hint of an explanation. Although she found nothing of note, Linda continued to "stew" over what she took to be to be a snub. She imagined that Jen was angry with her for some reason, or that "Jen was just tired of me as a friend." At times, Linda felt angry with Jen, and heard herself thinking, "How *dare* Jen do this to me, after all we've been through?" Linda wanted to call Jen for some kind of explanation, but was too hurt and embarrassed. Several weeks went by, and Linda became increasingly despondent. Finally, two weeks before the wedding, Jen phoned Linda to apologize for "the major screw-up with the invitations." Jen explained that the wrong card had gone out to Linda who was, of course, one of the bridesmaids.

This vignette is an example not only of how our "judgment" or interpretation of events shapes our feelings, but also a cautionary tale: when we reach judgments based on unfounded speculation, we often pay the price. Linda might well have been spared weeks of hurt feelings if she had simply withheld judgment or entertained alternative possibilities; for example, "Maybe the real invitation got lost in the mail . . . or maybe Jen mixed up the cards. And anyway, suppose Jen *didn't* choose me to be a bridesmaid. What's so horrible about that? Maybe she has some close relatives who would feel really hurt if she didn't choose them. It wouldn't necessarily mean she no longer values me as a friend."

In the Old Testament, we are admonished, "In justice you shall judge your neighbor" (Leviticus 19:15). And in the *Talmud*, we are taught, "Be cautious in judgment," (Pirke Avot 1:1) and, "Judge all individuals charitably" (Pirke Avot 1:6). In the Christian tradition, Thomas a Kempis warns us, "In judging others . . . we are often mistaken . . . our judgment is frequently influenced by our personal feelings, and it is very easy to fail in right judgment when we are inspired by private motives" (1995, 35). The Stoics go even further in their analysis of judgment, especially when judging others. Marcus Aurelius asks, "Does another do me wrong? Let him look to it" (97), and adds, "Our perturbations come only from the opinion which is within" (54).

Rabbi Zelig Pliskin describes a group in Israel that meets on a regular basis and tries to come up with "excuses" for slights that group members have suffered. As quoted by Rabbi Joseph Telushkin (2006, 35), here is one example:

> You were hoping that somebody would invite you to his house, but he failed to do so.
> **a.** Perhaps someone in his family is ill.
> **b.** Perhaps he was planning to be away from home
> **c.** Perhaps he did not have enough food in his house.

In short, happiness is largely (though not entirely) a function of how charitably, calmly, and accurately we *judge* things—not of things in themselves. And when we feel "hurt" by things or events, we need to look inward toward the opinions we have formed about these externals.

~

There is a tale told of Epictetus, who—as a young man—was held as a slave. When his master once put his leg in a torturous position, Epictetus calmly remarked, "You will break my leg." When this actually happened, he added—with equal composure—"Did I not tell you so?" (Bonforte, vii).

But Rabbi Joseph Telushkin takes exception to the classic Stoic view that anger is always inappropriate. He writes,

> Philo's and Seneca's reasoning strikes me as unreasonable. For example, those who were infuriated by Hitler, such as Winston Churchill, were more apt to want to fight and destroy him than those who were not particularly angry. . . . For that matter, who would want to live in a city whose police department was composed of officers who felt no anger toward the murderers, rapists, and pederasts they were trying to catch? As Rabbi Abraham Joshua Heschel has written: "[Anger's] complete suppression in the face of outbursts of evil may amount to surrender and capitulation. . . The complete absence of anger stultifies moral sensibility." (Telushkin 2006)

Rabbi Telushkin and Rabbi Heschel raise excellent points. Rather than suppressing one's anger entirely in the face of a monstrous evil, it is probably wiser to permit oneself just enough anger to get the job done. And what is the job? To defeat the evil—not to bring on apoplexy! Indeed, allowing oneself to be overcome by rage *also stultifies moral sensibility.*

~

Everything has two handles—one by which it may be borne, another by which it cannot. If your brother acts unjustly, do not lay hold on the affair by the handle of his injustice, for by that it cannot be borne; but rather, by the opposite: that he is your brother, that he was brought up with you; and thus, you will lay hold on it as it is to be borne.

—Epictetus (Bonforte, 84).

Eva was a 45-year-old dance instructor who had been married to George—a computer scientist—for the past 20 years. Although Eva described George as "a very decent guy," she also found him difficult to talk to. "He tries to listen, but it's like he just goes through the motions. There's no *there* there," Eva complained. George had also been quite unsupportive of Eva's attempts to start her own dance studio, a venture that he considered "impractical" and "self-indulgent." He urged Eva to find a job that brought in a "reliable income." Eva and George had been to a well-respected marriage counselor, and for a few years, things seemed better, according to Eva. But recently, George had begun to feel that the marriage was "no longer working" for him. He gently but unequivocally told Eva that he wanted a divorce. The two of them agreed to part ways amicably, and Eva got her own apartment in a nearby town. She seemed to do quite well for the first few weeks, but shortly thereafter, Eva began to feel "old, ugly, and unloved." She began to wonder " . . . how George could have dumped me, just like that! What was wrong with me? Was I too stupid? Was I *that* unattractive? How *dare* he do this to me!" Eva began to eat excessively, sleep 10–12 hours a day, and neglect her personal hygiene. She decided to see a psychotherapist to deal with her feelings of depression and self-deprecation.

In Epictetus' terms, we might say that Eva has grasped the break-up of her marriage by "the wrong handle." Of course, we can well understand how such a loss would be an occasion for *sadness* on the part of both Eva and George. But Eva came to see the break-up in terms of her own worth and attractiveness, rather than as the unfortunate outcome of divergent goals and temperaments. What might have been the "other handle" in this case? Eva might have reasoned with herself as follows: "Well, I'm very sad to see our marriage fall apart, and there's no denying it. But it looks as if we were just not meant to be together. George is a nice guy, but he doesn't seem able to meet my emotional needs, or give me much in the way of support for the things that mean a lot to me. As hard as this is, maybe the divorce is a blessing in disguise. Maybe it's an opportunity for me to do the kind of 'dance' in life I've always wanted to do—start my own studio, strike out on my own. Who knows? Maybe there's somebody else out there for me—a real soul mate! But even if I'm on my own, that's OK—I can make it."

Nobody would pretend that it's easy to grasp the "right handle" when life presents us with misfortune. And yet, Epictetus' teaching is a cornerstone not only of Stoicism, but of various spiritual traditions as well. For example, in the Hasidic tradition of Judaism, we find this teaching from the Baal Shem Tov (1700–1760), the founder of Hasidism: "Before [every individual] is always an element of good and an element of bad . . . [he or she] needs to isolate the bad aspect and reject it, whilst isolating and strengthening the good element" (Besserman, 142). This, too, means grasping the "right handle."

∼

Buddhism and Stoicism

There are many affinities between several Stoic beliefs and those of Buddhism—though the latter is so diverse, it's hard to make generalizations. Nevertheless, this passage by a scholar of religion makes clear some of the similarities:

> *Buddhist teaching focuses on three fundamental qualities of all things. . . . The first is hardship or suffering; the second, impermanence. Nobody is immune to sadness and disappointment. No one has a lock on success and genuine contentment. And everything comes to an end. Everything. The third quality . . . is*

the notion that there is no permanent, indestructible core or "soul" at the center of any being . . . [The] Buddha was not attempting to empty life of its meaning. He wanted people to change their minds about what matters most. Look hard at what motivates you. . . . Probe deeply into your choices and you will see that what you are really looking for you cannot get from this possession or that person. . . . [It] is a serious mistake to treat your world as though it existed for you." (Renard 2004, 318)

Teachings of the Buddha

Friends, I know nothing which brings suffering as does an untamed, uncontrolled, unattended and unrestrained heart. Such a heart brings suffering. Friends, I know of nothing which brings joy as does a tamed, controlled, attended and restrained heart. Such a heart brings joy. (from the Anguttara Nikaya, *translated by G. Fronsdal; in Kornfield 1993, 86)*

~

It is not he who gives abuse . . . who offends us; but the view that we take of these things, as insulting or hurtful. When, therefore, any one provokes you, be assured that it is your own opinion which provokes you. Try therefore, in the first place, not to be bewildered by appearances. For, if you once gain time for thought, you will more easily command yourself.

—Epictetus, LXXX (Bonforte, 94).

Burt, a 50-year-old automobile assembly line supervisor, believed in "instant justice." He explained this as follows: "When someone in my work crew gives me grief, or starts mouthing off about me, I get right in his face as soon as it happens. I nip it in the bud and that's that." But this mindset had landed Burt in trouble on more than one occasion. For example, one of Burt's supervisees once made a comment to a co-worker that Burt happened to overhear from some distance. The actual comment was, "Watch out—Burt puts the screws to you when you mess up." But Burt thought the man had said, "Burt purposely screws you when you mess up." Burt had responded by accosting the supervisee and making, in Burt's words, "a pretty ugly scene. I was all over this guy and almost punched him out. Then a couple of my crew came over and told me what this guy had actually said, which wasn't so bad. I mean, I pride myself on putting the screws to people when they mess up, but I'm fair about it. I wound up getting in trouble with my boss for losing my cool."

We have already discussed Marcus Aurelius's comment that "things do not touch the soul, for they are external and remain immovable; but our perturbations come only from the opinion which is within." Epictetus—who lived a generation before Marcus—makes two important points that presage and already go further than Marcus's teaching. First, he observes that we are often "bewildered by appearances." The notion that things are not always as they seem goes back at least to the philosophy of Plato (427–347 BC) and his famous "Parable of the Cave." In trying to convey how imperfectly we perceive reality, Plato evoked the image of a group of people trapped in a cave whose only knowledge of the outside world came from watching the movements of shadows cast on the wall. Similarly, in the Hindu tradition, we find the concept of *maya*, sometimes defined as "the theory of cosmic illusion" (Hume, 38). Basically, *maya* tells us that our senses and impressions often mislead us—or at least, that they disclose only the superficial aspects of reality. Epictetus is urging us to see beyond and beneath our first impressions—whether those stem from an overheard conversation or a snap judgment we make about someone we've just met.

The second great teaching from Epictetus is that " . . . if you once *gain time* for thought, you will more easily command yourself." Jumping to conclusions on the basis of meager evidence—as Burt did—often leads us to a loss of self-control. We need to take a deep breath when we find ourselves angry, study all the available evidence, and think carefully about what is actually happening. Similarly, in the *Talmud*, we are told, "Be cautious in judgment . . ." (Pirke Avot 1:1). On this point, Rabbi Shlomo Toperoff warns us, "A shallow judgment can do an incalculable amount of harm" (Toperoff, 21).

~

Dealing with Anger

Seneca asks, "What's the use . . . of mastering a horse and controlling him with the reins at full gallop if you're carried away yourself by totally unbridled emotions? What's the use of overcoming opponent after opponent in the wrestling or boxing rings if you can be overcome by your temper?" (Letter LXXXVIII, Campbell, 156).

The Rabbis taught that there are three ways you can gauge the character of an individual: by how generous he or she is; by how much the person drinks; and by how he or she expresses anger. In Proverbs, we are told, "A soft answer turns away anger" (15:1). Rabbi Lori Forman adds, "The next time you come up against anger, see if you can respond with a soft or gentle word to disarm its acceleration" (Olitzky & Forman, 26).

And—if you must be angry—learn the proper time and manner in which to express it. As Nachman of Bratslav put it: "I conquered my hostility by putting it away until the day I might need it."

Who Is Mighty?

The Book of Proverbs tells us, "One who controls his passions is better than one who conquers a city" (16:32). Rabbi Joseph Telushkin cites a relatively modern parable that illustrates this. He notes that John Jay (1743–1829), the first chief justice of the U.S. Supreme Court, lost the 1792 gubernatorial race in New York. After his defeat, he wrote the following to his wife: "A few more years will put us all in the dust, and it will then be of more importance to me to have governed myself than to have governed the state" (Telushkin 2006, 54).

NOTE

1. Psychiatrists would add an important caveat in this regard: in cases of serious depression, there are almost always genetic, biological and chemical factors contributing to the problem. In many such cases, appropriate medication can help the individual feel better. For an excellent, "reader-friendly" discussion of the biological side of things, I highly recommend Dr. John Medina's book, *Depression: How It Happens, How It's Healed* (New Harbinger Publications, 1998).

Chapter Two

Mortality and Meaning

"Since it is possible that you may depart from life this very moment, regulate every act and thought accordingly."

—Marcus Aurelius (Long, 25)

[T]he one who lives longest and the one who will die soonest lose just the same.

—Marcus Aurelius (Long, 29)

Our American culture does not deal very well with the issue of death. We rarely speak of loved ones who have "died"—rather, they have "passed away" or "passed on." The writer Ernest Becker once described how the "denial of death" permeates our lives. And yet, if we are not willing to embrace the inevitability of our own deaths, we may never be able to seize our own lives. Nor will we be able to experience the poignancy and dignity of our shared human condition. I believe this was implicit in President John F. Kennedy's speech at American University in June 1963, when he spoke of "our most basic common link[s] . . . We all cherish our children's future. And we are all mortal."

Shakespeare, in his play, *Cymbeline*, put it this way:

> Golden lads and girls all must,
> As chimney-sweepers, come to dust.
> The scepter, learning, physic must
> All follow this and come to dust. (IV.II)

And the Stoics recognized that a keen awareness of death gives us the opportunity *to create meaning in our lives*. The idea of living as if "you may

11

depart from life this very moment" may strike you as a little morbid. But re-member—Marcus Aurelius was an emperor! He did not have time to sit around and brood about death. Rather, he transformed his awareness of death's ever-present possibility into a reason for living life to the full. This didn't mean "eat, drink, and be merry"—it meant living a life of integrity and value.

And although it often strikes us as "cruel" when a young and promising life is cut short, the Stoics remind us that—in the larger scheme of eternity—there is little difference between "the one who lives longest" and "the one who will die soonest." This is a hard concept for many of us to accept, since we are conditioned to think in terms of *longevity* rather than *depth and quality* of life. But a hundred or a thousand years from now, it will make little difference whether you or I lived to age 35 or 95. On the other hand, it might make a considerable difference if, in our lives, we performed many acts of kindness, or left behind a cure for cancer, or a book of poems that comforts generations to follow.

Marcus has a hard truth to teach us—one, in fact, that only a few will ever really take to heart. He says that the individual "of trained reason" waits for death "as one of the natural functions; and, as you now wait for the unborn child to come forth from your wife's womb, so expect the hour in which your soul will drop from this shell" (Farquharson, 64). Or, as the great French es-sayist, Michel de Montaigne, was to put it many centuries later, "I want death to find me planting my cabbages, neither worrying about it, nor the unfin-ished gardening" (Essays I.20, in de Botton, 155).

～

A life is never incomplete if it is an honorable one. At whatever point you leave life, if you leave it in the right way, it is a whole.
　　　　　　　　　　　　　　—Seneca *(Letter LXXVII; Campbell, 125)*

The recent untimely death of newsman Peter Jennings prompted many thoughts, among his colleagues, concerning mortality, longevity, and the no-tion of living "the good life." The Nightline crew commented as follows: "It's a sad day throughout the halls of ABC News, but also a day to celebrate a rich and accomplished life."

～

Wait for [death] as one of the operations of nature. As you now wait for the time when the child shall come out of your wife's womb, so be ready for the time when your soul shall fall out of this envelope . . .
　　　　　　　　　　　　　　—Marcus Aurelius (G. Long, 192).

That which has died falls not out of the universe. If it stays here, it also changes here, and is dissolved into its proper parts, which are elements of the universe and of yourself. And these too change, and they murmur not.

—Marcus Aurelius (G. Long, 168).

The Stoic philosophers are perhaps least convincing when dealing with the issues of death, dying, and grief. For example, Marcus Aurelius calls grief "a mark of weakness"—which it surely is not! And yet, properly applied, there are elements of Stoic philosophy that are capable of consoling us in the face of our mortality—and even in the face of great loss. This is nicely brought out in a case described by Dr. Lou Marinoff (*Therapy for the Sane*, 2003). He describes a young woman who had lost her husband in the attack of September 11, 2001. "Michaela," Marinoff writes, "was inconsolable. A year later, she still kept Ron's clothing hanging in his closet, left his personal effects untouched in his den, and wouldn't change the pillowcases, which still bore his scent. She cried herself to sleep every night, hugging the pillow as if it were Ron himself."

Clearly, this tragic situation does not call for glib advice to "Pull yourself out of it!" or "Just move on!" Almost invariably, such comments only sharpen the pain of those who are grieving—perhaps beyond healthy bounds, as in this case. Some individuals who develop a *major depressive episode* after the loss of a loved one may require psychotherapy and even antidepressant medication, in severe cases. But some people simply need help in moving beyond the paralysis of their grief—and in this regard, Stoic philosophy *used appropriately* may be of help.

Thus, Marinoff describes how this worked for Michaela:

First and foremost, the key to Michaela's recovery is that she did not hate the terrorists who murdered her husband, nor did she hate God for taking him away from her. Absent hatred, a terrible poison, her hellish state of mind was much more amenable to being changed into something better. Whereas hatred blinds us, sadness can open our eyes . . . Second, by facing and owning her sadness through calm meditation and reflection on the *attachments that cause suffering*, Michaela began to realize and accept that Ron was gone for good. Sleeping with his ghost (e.g., his scented pillowcase), trying to love it . . . was actually a way of torturing herself and prolonging her agony. Instead, Michaela could learn to accept that Ron's life had been very beautiful, and that she had been most fortunate to share a few wonderful years with him . . . Once she let [Ron] go, she could remember their love with joy and sadness but without torment. (135–36, emphasis mine).

The notion that certain "attachments" cause suffering is both a Stoic and a Buddhist concept—and also has resonances in Hindu and Judaic teachings (see Pies 2000). Indeed, Buddhism tells us that there are two roots of unhappiness in human existence: there is *dukha*, which is the inevitable unhappiness that comes with human suffering, frailty, disease, loss of loved ones, and of course, death. And there is *tanha*, which is translated as "blind demandingness." E.A. Burtt describes *tanha* as that part of our nature "which leads us to ask of the universe . . . more than it is ready or even able to give" (Burtt 1982, 28). For example, asking God or Fate or the Universe never to take away those we love is a form of *tanha*. It is by no means easy to part with such attachment—but when we do, we often find that the bitter taste of our grief begins to dissipate.

In this regard, we would do well to recall Shakespeare's words: "All that lives must die, Passing through nature to eternity" (Hamlet I.ii.72). And finally, we find a very similar sentiment expressed in the *Talmud*: "Death is the haven of life, and old age the ship which enters the port" (Lankevich, 47).

~

Cicero (106 B.C.–43 B.C.) on Old Age

The course of life is fixed, and nature admits of its being run but in one way, and only once; and to each part of our life there is something specially seasonable; so that . . . the high spirit of youth, the soberness of maturer years, and the ripe wisdom of old age—all have a certain natural advantage which should be secured in its proper season.

[Nevertheless] . . . we must stand up against old age and make up for its drawbacks by taking pains . . . We must look after our health, use moderate exercise, take just enough food and drink to recruit, but not to overload, our strength. Nor is it the body alone that must be supported, but the intellect and soul much more. For they are like lamps: unless you feed them with oil, they too go out from old age. . . .

[T]he intellect becomes nimbler by exercising itself. For what Cæcilius means by "old dotards of the comic stage" are the credulous, the forgetful, and the slipshod. These are faults that do not attach to old age as such, but to a sluggish, spiritless, and sleepy old age. The fact is that old age is respectable just as long as it asserts itself, maintains its proper rights, and is not enslaved to any one. (translation from The Harvard Classics 1909, 14).

Great deeds are not done by strength or speed or physique: they are the products of thought, and character, and judgment. And far from diminishing, such qualities actually increase with age" (Cicero, trans. Michael Grant 1971, 220).

A Meditation on Life

Michel de Montaigne (1533–92), arguably the greatest confessional essayist since St. Augustine, was profoundly influenced by the Stoics, particularly Seneca, (c. 4–65 CE) the great Roman philosopher and playwright. Yet Montaigne was suspicious of the emphasis given to "preparing for death" in some Stoic writings. Montaigne counsels us as follows:

> *Philosophy ordains that we should always have death before our eyes, to see and consider it before the time . . . [but] . . . If we have not known how to live, 'tis injustice to teach us how to die. . . . I never saw any peasant among my neighbors cogitate . . . [about how] . . . he should pass over his last hour; nature teaches him not to think of death till he is dying; and then he does it with a better grace than Aristotle. (From "On Physiognomy," accessed at the* Online Library of Liberty*)*

~

Another great philosopher heavily influenced by the Stoics, Baruch Spinoza (1632–77) put it this way: "The wise man thinks of death least of all things. His wisdom is a meditation on life." Or, as my family would say, lifting a glass of wine, "*L'chaim!*" ("To life!")

Chapter Three

Morality and Self-Respect

Never value anything as profitable to yourself which shall compel you to break your promise, to lose your self-respect, to hate anyone, to suspect, to curse, [or] to act the hypocrite

—Marcus Aurelius (Long, 42–3)

The Stoics believe that right is the only good . . . advantage can never conflict with right . . . Besides, the Stoics' ideal is to live consistently with nature. I suppose what they mean is this: throughout our lives, we ought invariably to aim at morally right courses of action, and . . . must select only those which do not clash with such courses.

—Cicero, *On Duties* (162–63)

In the movie, *In Good Company*, the main character, Dan Foreman (played by Dennis Quaid), refuses to sell his soul for the sake of personal power and corporate greed. In contrast, his much younger boss seems, at first, to embrace the dog-eat-dog philosophy we associate with big business these days. Yet by the end of the film, the younger man has absorbed some valuable lessons about life from the older.

The Roman statesman and writer Cicero (106–43 B.C.) would have understood Dan Foreman very well. Cicero suggests that *genuine* advantage can never really conflict with what is right. For whenever we *appear* to gain the upper hand by "sticking it" to the other guy, or by making a shady business deal, we actually lose the larger battle for our souls. Indeed, we are pitting ourselves against Nature itself—if, by "Nature," we understand the entire world of universal moral law and human values.

This concept of Nature and "natural law" may seem strange in our age of cultural relativism—when every moral value is reduced to some special interest group's "narrative" or "agenda." Yet when Thomas Jefferson wrote, in the Declaration of Independence, "We hold these truths to be self-evident, that all men are created equal, that they are endowed by their Creator with certain unalienable Rights," it was to just such a concept of Natural Law that he was appealing. Similarly, the great American philosopher Ralph Waldo Emerson spoke in distinctly Ciceronian terms when he said, " . . . in the soul of man there is a justice whose retributions are instant and entire. He who does a good deed is instantly ennobled. He who does a mean deed is by the action itself contracted. . . . If a man dissemble, deceive, he deceives himself and goes out of acquaintance with his own being" (in Lindeman, 167).

∼

For what shall it profit a man, if he shall gain the whole world, and lose his own soul?

—Matthew 16:26

Commenting on this famous passage from the New Testament, an unnamed writer associated with the Atma Jyoti Ashram says, "I have spent my entire life watching people gain a little bit of the world and lose their souls. And ultimately they lost the world, too, either in the changes of earthly fortune or through the finality of death." (http://www.atmajyoti.org/up_isha_upanishad_2.asp)

∼

I do my duty. Other things trouble me not.

—Marcus Aurelius (Long, 115)

Sarah had a troubled relationship with her mother. Despite Sarah's best efforts over many years, Sarah's mother never forgave her daughter for "leaving home so young and not settling down with a decent man." Actually, Sarah had not left home until college, but her mother had wanted her daughter to stay in their small town and help her run the family business, following the death of Sarah's father. Her mother had also voiced the view that Sarah should "settle down, get married, and raise a family close by." Sarah had other ideas—she went to college, and then got a master's degree in business administration. During her years away, Sarah made trips back home nearly every month, to help her mother deal with the business. After graduation from business school, Sarah arranged to spend six months back home, helping her mother deal with some complicated tax issues involving the family's small clothing store. She also helped her mother cope with a variety of medical problems, household repairs, and personal financial concerns. Despite all this, Sarah's mother seemed stand-offish and "whiny." She would not let Sarah off the hook for "leaving me all alone and high-tailing it out of town" years earlier.

Sarah was clearly someone with a strong sense of obligation and responsibility. Though she may have defied her mother's wishes years ago, Sarah was only choosing the life she thought best for herself. Now, she was doing everything she could to help her mother cope. In short, Sarah had "done her duty." Unfortunately, many of us fulfill our responsibilities, but still fall short of the expectations or hopes of others. And sometimes, despite our best efforts to help our loved ones, they get sick, fall into financial difficulty, or get in trouble with the law. Marcus Aurelius tells us that if we have done our duty, that is all we can rightly expect. Similarly, Epictetus tells us, "If you fulfill your duties, you have what belongs to you" (Bonforte, 73). What does he mean by this? I think Epictetus is telling us *that the only real possession to which we may lay claim is our own moral integrity.* Everything else in life either belongs to someone else, or is beyond our control.

Chapter Four

Adversity and Self-Possession

A wise man ought not to regret his struggles with fortune any more than a brave soldier should be intimidated by the noise of battle.

—Boethius, *Consolation of Philosophy* (Trans. Richard Green 1962, 99)

As Boethius also noted, "The only true joy is self-possession in the face of adversity" (27). The idea was expressed a bit more humorously by one wag, who said, "When life hands you lemons, ask for a bottle of tequila and salt." I don't really recommend that approach, but sometimes a good laugh does help puts things in perspective, and the Stoics were not renowned for their sense of humor

∼

Maimonides (1135–1204) on Self-Discipline

The more a man is disciplined, the less he is affected by both extremes, good times and bad; so that when he is favored by great fortune in this world . . . he does not get excited nor appear particularly great and good in his own eyes. And when great misfortune and tribulation befall him . . . he is neither startled not terrified, but tolerates them well.
—From The Preservation of Youth *(Trans. Hirsch L. Gordon; cited in Klagsbrun, 1990, pp. 30–31)*

The renowned medieval philosopher, theologian, and physician—known as Rambam— *had a great deal of experience with both good and bad fortune. The death at sea of his younger brother, David, is said to have left Maimonides*

19

disconsolate for many years. Yet his philosophy of emotional discipline must have served him well during his rich and troubled life

～

The art of living resembles wrestling more than dancing . . .
—Marcus Aurelius (Farquharson, 50)

Why wrestling? Marcus explains that in life, as in wrestling, we must stand "prepared and unshaken" to meet whatever comes our way. Easier said than done, of course.

Consider what happened to Fred, a 47-year-old computer programmer who was anticipating a promotion within the company he had served faithfully for more than 20 years. When the "technology bubble" burst, Fred's boss called him into the office and informed Fred that he was being offered a "retirement package." Fred was flabbergasted and angry—but he agreed to read over the proposal. It turned out that Fred was effectively being terminated from the company, with a very modest severance package.

For the first week or two, Fred went into an emotional tailspin. As he put it, "I just moped around the house, stayed in bed until noon, and barely ate a thing. Why bother going in to work? I was getting canned anyway." After Fred's wife pushed him to see a "job coach," Fred's spirits picked up. He decided to confront his boss and lobby for a better deal. When his boss indicated that "This is the best we can do," Fred hired a lawyer and informed his company he intended to fight the retirement package. The company decided to increase the severance package by more than 30%, allowing Fred to start his own very successful consulting firm.

Shakespeare reminds us that "Sweet are the uses of adversity . . . " (*As You Like It*, II. I.12). But more often than not, we must *wrestle* with adversity, in order to "wrest" from it some unexpected gift. The most famous instance of this was Jacob's wrestling with the Angel, described in Genesis 32:25–33. You may recall that the archangel, Michael, struggles all night long with Jacob, until at last, Michael begs Jacob to release him. Jacob replies, "I will not let you go until you bless me." The angel agrees to do so, and Jacob's name is changed to *Israel*, ". . . for you have striven with beings divine and human and have prevailed." Yet the battle was not without a cost—Jacob's "hip socket was wrenched at the thigh muscle" (Tanakh, 52).

The lesson from this parable, I believe, is that we must be prepared to "wrestle" with life—and with death—if we are to receive the blessings of personal growth and spiritual integrity. We may, indeed, be injured in the struggle—but it is often worth it.

~

Be Prepared

There is a reason for ensuring that nothing ever takes us by surprise. We should project our thoughts ahead of us at every turn and have in mind every possible eventuality instead of only the usual course of events . . . we should be anticipating not merely all that commonly happens but all that is conceivably capable of happening, if we do not want to be overwhelmed and struck numb by rare events . . .

—Seneca, Letter XCI (Campbell, 178–9)

I write this in the aftermath of Hurricane Katrina, and on the fourth anniversary of the September 11 terrorist attacks. It is almost incontestable that these events—though different in many respects—share the trait of having eluded productive anticipation. *I mean that neither event was anticipated in such a way as* to have *protected the American people. To be sure, some terrorism experts and intelligence sources had warned of something like the 9/11 attacks; and many experts on hurricanes and floods had envisioned the catastrophic effects of a severe hurricane upon New Orleans. But somehow, our imagination* failed to enlist our will. *And even in the face of articles written years before Katrina, virtually predicting the horrors that were to come, many "authorities" proffered excuses along the lines of, "Well, yes, we knew the levees might* overflow, *but we didn't anticipate they would actually* break." *The New York Times (9/11/05) reported that many residents of New Orleans had come to believe that the city was protected by God, and that a major hurricane would therefore veer away at the last minute! Seneca might have shaken his head sadly at these words, noting, "Misfortune has a way of choosing some unprecedented means or other of impressing its power on those who might be said to have forgotten it" (179).*

Strength just comes in one brand—you stand up at sunrise and meet what they send you, and keep your hair combed.

—Reynolds Price, in Kate Vaiden

~

The cucumber is bitter? Put it down. There are brambles in the path? Step to one side. That is enough, without also asking, 'Why did these things come into the world at all?'

—Marcus Aurelius, (Farquharson, 60)

Helen was a 67-year-old retired math teacher, who had lost her husband of some 40 years last fall. Ever since retirement two years ago, Helen had been brooding about how "unfair" life had been to her. "I always get the short end of the stick," she complained to a friend. "First of all, I didn't really want to retire, but my health was giving out, and I was told I wasn't keeping up with the work load. Then last November, Bill died, and the "nest egg" I thought we had accumulated all those years turned out to be next to nothing. Now I have to supplement my social security with tutoring, which I really don't enjoy. '*Why me?*' I keep asking myself." Helen found herself dwelling on Bill's death, but focusing mainly on how "unfair" it was that he had been "taken" from her.

To make matters worse, Helen had recently discovered a lump in her breast, and was now facing the frightening prospect of a biopsy and possible cancer. "It just seems like the world is stacked against me, and there's nothing I can do about it," she complained to her therapist. "If there's a God, He or She sure has a pretty rotten sense of humor!" Helen added bitterly.

As Rabbi Harold S. Kushner famously put it, sometimes "bad things happen to good people." Of course, most of us can empathize with Helen and even understand her bitterness. After all, she has had to deal with a number of major losses and frustrations. But most of us can say the same thing by the time we are Helen's age! Not everybody winds up chronically embittered, or complaining of getting the "short end of the stick." The plain truth is, we can torment ourselves with wondering why the world is so terribly "unfair," or we can take steps to correct the situation we find ourselves in—stepping to one side of the "brambles." Philosophy professor Lou Marinoff puts it this way:

> [D]oes it make sense to say, "I know I just lost my job, but I don't suffer from it"? Of course it does. You can mourn a lost job to be sure, but you can also view it as an opportunity to find a new and more suitable one. This applies to many kinds of loss. (Marinoff 2003, 139)

Indeed, we can even use the adversity in our lives to enhance our emotional growth and depth of character. This isn't easy, of course—it takes practice and discipline. The ancient rabbis tell us, "A broken heart prepares man for the service of God . . . " (Buber, cited in Besserman 1994, 185). They have in mind something along these lines: When we have suffered ourselves, we become better equipped to understand and relieve the suffering of others. And so, while few of us would willingly choose adversity, we need not reject it as a worthless burden imposed by an unfair God.

∽

Keep Your Mind Off Your Illness

Epicurus says, "In illness, my conversation was not about the suffering of my body, nor [did I] . . . talk to my visitors about such matters . . . [Rather,] I continued to debate leading principles of science . . . I did not even permit the medical men to give themselves airs, as though they were doing some great thing . . . [and thus] my life passed on happily and brightly" (Farquharson, 69).

Writing from the Buddhist perspective, Robert Thurman advocates a meditative approach to one's suffering: "Think about . . . the thousands of ways in which we can be knocked down by illness, pain, injury, sorrow, death. Why do we take this step now? Because meditation on the prevalence of suffering helps us tolerate our pains by putting them into perspective" (Thurman, 170).

How Much Grief is Too Much?

Seneca was hard-nosed but not utterly insensitive when it came to grief and mourning. He tells us, "We can be pardoned for having given way to tears so long as they have not run down in excessive quantities . . . Tears, yes, but not lamentation . . . Let us see to it that the recollection of those we have lost becomes a pleasure to us . . . " (Letter LXII, Campbell, 114).

Many psychologists and psychiatrists would disagree with Seneca on this point, arguing that "Each of us must find the right way to grieve . . . you can't put artificial limits on mourning." There is much truth in this, but there is also a solid kernel of truth to Seneca's idea that we must eventually find ways to limit grief. Without such limits, our lives are given over to the spirit of death. The 12th-century sage and physician Moses ben Maimon (Maimonides) also understood this. While Maimonides clearly felt that grief was appropriate after, say, the death of a loved one, he counseled against excessive or prolonged mourning. Thus, in his work, Mishneh Torah *(Hilkhot Avel 13:1), Maimonides advises "three days for weeping, seven days for lamenting, and thirty days for [abstaining] from cutting the hair" (Halkin and Hartman 291). More strikingly, he prescribes a well-defined behavioral procedure for 'weaning' the mourner from the grieving process:*

> *During the first three days, the mourner should think of himself as if a sword is resting upon his neck; from the third to the seventh day as if it is lying in the corner; thereafter, as if it is moving toward him in the street. Reflections of this nature will put him on his mettle, he will bestir himself. (292; Hilkhot Avel 13:12)*

In essence, this is a form of 'guided imagery' analogous to that used in the treatment of various phobic and post-traumatic disorders. The message is,

"Grief is okay, within certain reasonable bounds. But you must sometimes work to move beyond grief."

~

There is room for heroism, I assure you, in bed as anywhere else.
                              —Seneca, Letter LXXVIII (Campbell, 137)

No, Seneca does not have sexual prowess in mind, but rather the heroism one may show even in the face of severe illness. Consider the case of Lenny, a 55-year old architect who had been diagnosed with rheumatoid arthritis three years ago. Not only did the severe pain and swelling in his hands prevent Lenny from working, he found that his mood began to plummet as he became less and less able to function. "What good am I to anybody now?" Lenny complained to his wife. "Architecture is the only thing I've really ever done, or ever loved." Lenny became increasingly withdrawn and apathetic.

Seneca might reply to Lenny as he did to his own friend, Lucilius, who was suffering from a severe, chronic cough:

> It is your body, not your mind as well, that is in the grip of ill health . . . you may still give instruction and advice, listen and learn, inquire and remember. Besides, if you meet sickness in a sensible manner, do you really think you are achieving nothing? You will be demonstrating that even if one cannot always beat it, one can always bear an illness. There is room for heroism, I assure you, in bed as anywhere else. . . . There is something . . . open to you to achieve, and that is making the fight with illness a good one. . . . Be your own spectator . . . your own applauding audience. (Letter LXXVIII, 137).

Seneca knew whereof he spoke. As a life-long asthmatic, he once admitted that the only thing that held him back from suicide was the thought of his father's inability to bear the loss (Campbell, 7). And yet, at the time of his letters to Lucilius—in his mid-sixties—Seneca remained mentally, politically, and socially active. As for fears of encroaching death, Seneca says to Lucilius, "In a single day, there lies open to men of learning more than there ever does to the unenlightened in the longest of lifetimes" (Letter LXXVIII, 139).

~

Good fortune deceives; adverse fortune teaches.
                              —*Boethius,* The Consolation of Philosophy

Reckon on everything; expect everything.
                                                                    —*Seneca*

The next time you are feeling sorry for yourself and your "hard life," read the biographies of Boethius and Seneca. Boethius (c. 480–524 CE) was a Roman statesman and philosopher who tried to eliminate governmental corruption—and wound up imprisoned on undoubtedly false charges of conspiracy and "sacrilege." While in prison, Boethius managed to produce one of the most widely read philosophical works of the Middle Ages—The Consolation of Philosophy (Trans. Green 1962). From the depths of his isolation, Boethius wrote:

> What I am about to say is so strange that I scarcely know how to make my meaning clear. I am convinced that adverse fortune is more beneficial . . . than prosperous fortune. When Fortune seems kind, and seems to promise happiness, she lies . . . .but bad fortune frees [men] by making them see the fragile nature of happiness.

We may see bitterness in this, and who could blame the man? But was Boethius on to something? The next time you watch one of those television game shows and see the winner of a new car jumping up and down, screaming with joy—try to hear Boethius' cautioning voice.

Seneca had the misfortune of living at the time of the deranged Emperor Nero, whom Seneca had tutored. Like Boethius, Seneca found himself falsely accused of conspiracy, and was ordered by Nero to take his own life. (Nero, who had murdered his own mother and brother, would doubtless have killed Seneca had the philosopher not ended his own life.) Seneca remained unperturbed, commenting, "After murdering his mother and brother, it only remained for him to kill his teacher and tutor!" (de Botton 2000). When Seneca counseled, "Reckon on everything; expect everything," he spoke from deep and painful experience.

∼

> Every trouble that may come our way presses harder on the one who has turned tail and is giving ground.
>
> —Seneca, Letter XXVIII (Campbell, 136).

Kate was a chronic procrastinator. Although very bright and creative, Kate almost invariably put off the "hard stuff" until the deadline was nearly upon her, and then scrambled to finish on time. This problem came up in her professional and her personal life. At the office, where Kate worked as a copy editor for a large newspaper, she would put off the "fact-checking" part of her job until just hours before her boss needed the work. Kate was clever enough to get the work done most of the time, but on several occasions, she had to ask her boss for an extension—which did not improve the boss's mood or his confidence in Kate. In her personal life, too, Kate avoided the difficult decisions. Her husband had been urging her for years to work with him on creating a "living will" and a "health care proxy" document, but Kate kept putting it off. "It just makes me frantic even thinking about all that death stuff," Kate acknowledged to a close friend. This habitual avoidance had caused a good deal of friction with her husband, who interpreted Kate's procrastination as "not really giving a damn about our needs or our future."

Psychologists Albert Ellis and Robert Harper have put it this way:

> [I]t is very difficult for the average or even the above-average individual to keep fighting against his or her normal tendencies to give up easily on hard tasks, to put off till tomorrow what really should be done today. . . . All right, so it's hard. But [the work] still continually has to be done, if innumerable life responsibilities are to be adequately faced and solved. . . . And there *is* no other way. Avoid or cavil as you may, the piper must be paid. (Ellis and Harper, 149).

Ellis and Harper go on to make the perceptive observation that, in most cases, procrastination actually stems from an irrational *fear of failure.* Rather than tackle that big assignment, write that Great American Novel, or search for that desired partner, we make excuses to ourselves—all to disguise our underlying fear that we shall fail in the postponed endeavor. But, as Seneca realized, turning tail and running away only puts the "enemy" closer to our backs. Indeed, for Seneca, "the only safe harbour in this life's tossing, troubled sea is to refuse to be bothered about what the future will bring, and to stand ready and confident, squaring the breast to take without skulking or flinching whatever fortune hurls at us" (Letter CIV, Campbell, 190).

Chapter Five

Perfectionism, Virtue, and Self-Acceptance

> Be not disgusted, nor discouraged, nor dissatisfied, if you do not succeed in doing everything according to right principles; but when you have failed, return back again . . .
>
> —Marcus Aurelius (Long, 86).

Louise was a 35-year old accountant with a long-standing weight problem. She had been on at least three different diet plans, none of which had worked for her. "I just couldn't stick to all the rules," she complained. Finally, on the fourth try, Louise succeeded in losing 15 pounds over the course of three months. She was ecstatic—until she and her husband took a three-week trip to Europe, where Louise proceeded to gain back six pounds. She came home thoroughly disgusted, "down on myself," and "feeling like a flop again."

Cognitive-behavioral therapists, using the Stoic perspective, would counsel Louise to go easier on herself, and "return back again" to her dieting efforts without condemning herself as a "flop." Everybody slips up now and then, the Stoics tell us. When that happens, we need to pick ourselves up, dust ourselves off, and get back to work.

This spirit of anti-perfectionism is also found in the Judaic tradition, as this passage from the *Talmud* suggests: "It is not up to you to complete the task, but you are not free to desist from it" (Pirke Avot 2:21). Similarly, in the Christian tradition, we find Thomas a Kempis saying, "Try as we will, we shall still fail all too easily in many things. Nevertheless, we should always have a firm resolve, especially against such faults as most hinder our progress" (1952, 49). And in the Hindu tradition, we are taught, "You must perform every action sacramentally, and be free from all attachment to results" (*Bhagavad Gita* 3:9, Browne, 105).

～

Thornton Wilder On Perfectionism

*To this day, many an American is breaking his life on an excessive demand
for the perfect, the absolute, and the boundless in realms where it is accorded
to few—in love and friendship, for example. The doctrines of moderation and
the golden mean may have flourished in Rome and in China . . . but they do
not flourish here, save as counsels of despair." (From lecture, "The American
Loneliness," given at Harvard and published in the* Atlantic Monthly, *August,
1952)*

Overcoming Fear of Failure

The Boston Globe *(5/13/05) ran a piece on two young Brandeis graduate stu-
dents whose passion for books and bookstores led them to an improbable venture: opening their own, independent bookstore, at a time when huge chain
stores are driving many such small-fry operations out of business. The* Globe
*headline read, "Risking failure, with enthusiasm," and the writer noted,
"Chutzpah they have . . . despite the long odds of succeeding." One of the two
owners, Alex Green, is quoted as saying, "What's the worst that can happen?
This is something we love and care about greatly. We're willing to take a
chance of failing."*

*Marcus Aurelius would have understood this bold resolve quite well. He
tells us, "If you work at that which is before you, following right reason seriously . . . calmly, without allowing anything else to distract you, but keeping your divine part pure . . . if you hold to this, expecting nothing, fearing
nothing, but satisfied with your present activities according to nature . . .
you will live happy" (Long, 47). And, should all go well, Marcus adds,
"Receive wealth or prosperity without arrogance, and be ready to let it
go" (174).*

*We find something of this serene determination and "chutzpah" in the
American sage, Ralph Waldo Emerson. He writes, "Do not follow where the
path may lead. Go instead where there is no path and leave a trail." And, for
those times when things don't go as planned, Emerson writes, "Character is
that which can do without success."*

～

It is the action of an uninstructed person to reproach others for his own misfortune; of one entering upon instruction to reproach himself; and of one perfectly
instructed, to reproach neither others nor himself.
—Epictetus (Bonforte, 92)

Consider the office of Meta-Life, a busy insurance company. Three members of the long-term disability team have been working together for the past few years. Rhonda is a bright 25-year-old fresh out of business school. She's a hard-working, responsible person, but has a singularly annoying habit: whenever there's a problem with a claim, somebody else is always at fault. If a claimant's folder is missing a vital piece of information, Rhonda is quick to point out that another employee "should have taken care of that." If a claimant becomes angry over the phone, Rhonda's response is always the same: "That guy is a complete jerk." Russ—a "thirty-something" colleague of Rhonda's—has just the opposite tendency. Whenever anything goes wrong, Russ takes the blame. When a claimant sued the company over a supposedly wrongful denial of claim, Russ fell on his sword. "If I had handled the case differently," he said, shaking his head sadly, "we wouldn't be in this mess." Typically, Russ would slide into a few days of depression after a "screw-up" like this. Rose was a 54-year old supervisor who worked closely with Rhonda and Russ. Rose was the sort of person you'd want around in a crisis—she always handled things calmly, efficiently, and without pointing the finger of blame. Rather than assign guilt when something went wrong, Rose would ask, "OK, how can we learn from this case? What can we do better in the future?" If Rose needed to discipline a recalcitrant claims analyst, she would always do so privately, and with respect for the person's feelings.

As you can readily see, Rhonda, Russ, and Rose represent, respectively, the three levels of "instruction" to which Epictetus refers. You might be objecting at this point that, without assigning blame, nothing would ever change or improve. But this highlights the difference between *reproach*—with its moral implications of rebuke and censure—and *assigning responsibility*. Rose is clearly willing to do the latter. Of course, there are instances in which we justifiably find fault with ourselves or others—and the Stoic view of Epictetus should not be construed as license to "do anything" without repercussion. Rather, the Stoic attitude *tempers* our moral judgments with the wisdom of the human condition and all its foibles—the knowledge that it is best to "Forbear to judge, for we are sinners all" (Shakespeare, *Henry VI, Part Two*, III.iii.31). Another way of understanding Epictetus' teaching is expressed in Pirke Avot, the ethical treatise of the *Talmud*. There we are told, "*Be cautious in judgment*" (Pirke Avot 1:1). According to Rabbi S. Toperoff, this teaching "advises us to be cautious and *not to judge a person lightly*; there may be extenuating circumstances which prompted the individual to act as he did. A Shallow judgment can do an incalculable amount of harm" (21, italics added).

And this is true with respect to both others *and ourselves*. For example, while it is the mark of maturity to accept responsibility for one's errors, it is the sign of wisdom to do so without self-loathing. Often there are "extenuating circumstances" that explain why we acted inappropriately or incompetently—perhaps we were sick, or deprived of sleep, or under tremendous emotional stress. These mitigating factors must not serve as *excuses* or cop-outs—rather, they should induce us to learn from our mistakes, and to try harder the next time. As the Book of Proverbs tells us, "He who ignores instruction despises himself, but he who heeds admonition gains understanding" (15:32).

Rose would undoubtedly agree.

~

Striking the Right Balance in How We See Ourselves

Marcus Aurelius tells us, "Little the life each lives, little the corner of the earth he lives in, little even the longest fame hereafter . . . " (Farquharson, 15). And he adds—in his usual unvarnished manner—"in a little while, you will be no one and nowhere" (Farquharson, 53). These sentiments may be seen as a counterbalance to those of the preceding section, in which we are admonished to revere ourselves as aspects of the Divine. There is no contradiction between these contrasting views of man. We are irreducibly divided beings—at once eternal and evanescent, divinity and dust. Montaigne put all this more earthly: "Upon the highest throne in the world, we are seated, still, upon our arses" (in de Botton, 126).

This paradox should lead us to a kind of internal equipoise—a position of neither self-loathing nor arrogance, neither despair nor grandiosity. In the Judaic tradition, we find the same paradox, and the same attempt at resolution. For example, in Pirke Avot (3.1), we are told,

> *Concentrate on three things and you will not fall into the grip of sin. Know from where you came, where you are going, and before Whom you will have to give account and reckoning. From where you came—from a putrid drop. Where you are going—to a place of dust, worms, and maggots. And before Whom you will have to give account and reckoning—before the Supreme King of kings, the Holy One, blessed be He.*

This is pretty sobering stuff! And yet, we should not bludgeon ourselves with the knowledge of our own limitations. Here is what the Hasidic master, Bunam of Przysucha, taught:

> *Each person should have two pockets. In each pocket, he or she should carry a slip of paper on which is written one of these two citations. As the occasion arises, one should extract and read the slip appropriate to the specific situation. If one becomes too haughty and proud, one should be aware that "I am dust and ashes"; and if one becomes too self-abusing and depressed, then one*

should extract the slip that reads, "For my sake the world was created."
(quoted in Sherwin & Cohen, 88)

~

What progress, you ask, have I made? I have begun to be a friend to myself.
> —Seneca, quoting the philosopher Hecato, in a letter to a friend
> (de Botton, 103).

Marcie was a 50-year old assistant vice-president at a large biotechnology firm. She was, by all objective standards, a very successful woman: she had not only moved into a high position at her firm, she had also managed to raise a family, cultivate a rich cultural life as a concert pianist, and carry out numerous charitable activities at her synagogue. And yet, Marcie described herself as "kind of a flop . . . I mean, I haven't done nearly the things I'm capable of doing. By now, I should be a senior vice-president, at least. As far as my music goes, I'm strictly county-fair level. If I had really applied myself, I might have been a real pianist. And family—forget it! I should be spending a lot more time with my kids than I do. I barely get to see my daughter perform in her dance class, I never do things with my son . . . and, frankly, my husband would probably not have much good to say about our sex life these days."

Actually, Marcie had won several local music awards for her performances, and was described by her kids as "a pretty cool Mom . . . We know we can count on her." Her husband, Ed, had "no complaints on the physical side of things," and felt that he and Marcie had "a really good marriage and family life."

Montaigne tells us, "The most uncouth of our afflictions is to despise our being" (*Essays*, III.13). And although there is a strain of self-abnegation that appears in the literature of Stoicism, there are also many statements concerning the importance of what psychologists sometimes call "positive self-regard." At the very least, we are not to torment ourselves with self-deprecation! Marcus tells us, "I do not deserve to give myself pain, for I never deliberately gave another pain" (Farquharson, 58). He adds, "Don't be disgusted, don't give up, don't be impatient if you do not carry out entirely conduct based in every detail upon right principles" (Farquharson, 29). And, on a more spiritual note, Marcus reminds us that, "every individual's mind is of God" (Farquharson, 92), and therefore is worthy of reverence and respect.

We find very similar sentiments expressed in the *Talmud*; e.g., "Do not consider yourself wicked" (Pirkei Avot 2:18). The Hasidic rebbe Nachman of Breslov (1771–1810) tells us, "Rather than falling into despair over his shortcomings, [Man] must seek out positive elements in the totality of his being and judge himself favorably on that basis" (Lieber, 27). And finally, in the very secular philosophy of Rational Emotive Therapy, as developed by Albert Ellis, we are told: "If human beings have any intrinsic worth or value, they have it by virtue of their mere existence, their *being*, rather than because of anything they do to 'earn' it. . . . You are 'good' or 'deserving' just because you *are*."

In short, "Give yourself a break!"

∿

Don't hope for Plato's Utopia, but be content to make a very small step forward and reflect that the result even of this is not trifling.
　　　　　—*Marcus Aurelius,* Meditations, *Book IX (Farquharson, 67)*

We often torment ourselves for having failed to achieve something which, examined in retrospect, was probably wildly unrealistic or grandiose. We seldom give ourselves credit for the small steps we take each day in pursuit of our goals and dreams. In the Judaic literature, there is a strong tradition of taking "partial credit" for one's efforts, and avoiding utopian goals. In his Commentary on Pirkei Avot (2:21), the Marharal of Prague tells us, "Studying Torah is not like building a house, which has no value unless it is complete. It is comparable to sowing seeds; every seed sown is a completed task, regardless of whether one finishes the entire field" (Basser, 138–39). And an even more eloquent renunciation of utopian goals is provided by Chaim of Zans:

In my youth, when I was fired with the love of God, I thought I would convert the whole world to God. But soon I discovered that it would be quite enough to convert the people who lived in my town, and I tried for a long time, but did not succeed. Then I realized that my program was still much too ambitious, and I concentrated on the persons in my own household. But I could not convert them either. Finally, it dawned on me: I must work upon myself, so that I may give true service to God. But I did not accomplish even this." (Trans. Martin Buber, cited in Besserman, 116)

∿

To the best of your ability . . . conduct inquiries of your own into all the evidence against yourself. Play the part first of prosecutor, then of judge, and finally of pleader in mitigation. Be harsh with yourself at times.
　　　　　—Seneca, Letter XXVIII (Campbell, 78)

Brett was a "thirty-something" publicist for a large Hollywood firm catering to celebrities. As a teenager, Brett had experienced bouts of depression and low self-esteem. He had seen a counselor who believed in "unconditional positive self-regard," and who had urged young Brett to "accept himself no matter what" his shortcomings. This idea did help Brett to emerge from his adolescent depression—but it also seemed to prolong his adolescence in some ways. At work, Brett almost never looked critically at his own performance. If something went wrong with a client, Brett would usually shrug, make a joke, and say something like, "Hey, some days you eat the bear, some days the bear eats you!" This "don't sweat it" attitude helped Brett cope with the normal ups and downs of professional work, but it also left him unwilling to ask the hard questions of himself, for example: "Is there something in my failures that points to a *pattern*? Is there something about me that needs to change before I can become more successful?" Although his co-workers liked Brett, his boss found Brett's nonchalance annoying at times, and told him as much.

As we have seen, self-esteem is important—and yet, it is not the whole story in the matter of our development as decent human beings. In the Judaic tradition, there is an act called *heshbon ha-nefesh*, first detailed by Rabbi Mendel of Satanov. Roughly translated, it means, "making an account of the state of one's soul." This is a kind of moral inventory the individual is encouraged to take periodically (not just during the "days of Judgment," such as Rosh Hashonah or Yom Kippur). Seneca is urging us to do something like this—starting with the hard questions; proceeding to the phase of self-judgment; and concluding with self-acceptance. Simply berating oneself is not helpful. We must be *fair* with ourselves—and that means seeing ourselves realistically but compassionately.

~

Practice even the things which you despair of achieving. For even the left hand, which for other uses is slow from want of practice, has a stronger hold upon the bridle than the right; for it has been practiced in this.
     —Marcus Aurelius, *Meditations,* Book XII (Farquharson, 89)

Kirk was a 43-year-old bank vice president. Though very successful in his work and happy in his family life, Kirk let an unfulfilled desire eat away at his self-esteem: he had always wanted to be a concert pianist. Although he did play the piano at home, and occasionally for his church, Kirk berated himself for "betraying my greatest dream." As a result of his self-contempt and bitterness, Kirk never applied himself to improving his skills as a pianist. "What's the point?" he would say to his wife, "I'm never going to reach the level where I could play professionally. I'm just knocking my head against the wall!"

A more rational and Stoic attitude would have served Kirk far better. He might have said to himself, "Okay, so I won't be playing at Carnegie Hall and I won't be the next Vladamir Horowitz. So what? I can still be a decent pianist, and I can improve my skills insofar as my time and obligations permit." As Ellis and Harper put it, "If you inordinately strive for success and are terribly afraid of failing, you will almost inevitably . . . fear taking chances, making mistakes . . . or doing what you would really like to do in life. . . . [I]nsisting on outstanding or perfect achievement . . . foredooms you not only to failure but to fear of failing—which has more pernicious effects than failure itself" (94).

~

When you run [up] against someone's wrong behavior, go on at once to reflect what similar wrong act of your own there is . . . for if you attend to this, you will quickly forget your anger.
        —Marcus Aurelius, *Meditations,* Book X (Farquharson, 76)

Jan was a 34 year-old mother of two who was constantly getting into arguments over "discipline" with her 14-year-old daughter, Britney. One day, while cleaning, Jan found a small stash of marijuana cigarettes in Britney's room. Later that day, livid with anger, Jan waved the bag of "joints" in front of Britney's face. She accused her daughter of being "a spoiled druggie who doesn't give a damn about anybody else." Britney tearfully replied, "Didn't you tell me once that you used to smoke a joint now and then when you were in college? You're a real hypocrite, Mom!" Stunned by this accusation, Jan withdrew quietly to her room. After reflecting on her daughter's comment, and on her own past behavior, Jan apologized to Britney for her outburst. This led to a much calmer discussion of drug use and its risks.

In the Gospel of John (8:7), we find the parable of the woman "caught in adultery" and about to be stoned. Jesus says to the crowd, "Let him who is without sin among you be the first to throw a stone at her" (*Oxford Annotated Bible*). The Stoic view advocated by Marcus is in a similar vein. Other religious traditions echo this spirit of tolerance; e.g., in Buddhism, the *Dhammapada* tells us, "It is easy to see the faults of others, but difficult to see one's own" (Mascaro, 71–2). And the *Talmud* encourages us to "judge all individuals charitably" (Pirke Avot 1:6). The advice given by Marcus, of course, adds a "practical" (if not self-interested) dimension to such charitable thinking—we wind up feeling less angry.

Chapter Six

Living in Harmony with the Universe

Nothing will happen to me which is not conformable to the nature of the universe.

—Marcus Aurelius (Long p. 89)

Frank was a 78-year-old retired engineer who prided himself on his independence and "toughness." His wife had died five years earlier, and Frank lived alone, with occasional visits from his daughter. A former marine, Frank had been in robust good health until about 9 months ago, when he suffered a serious stroke. This left him unable to talk for nearly a month, and barely able to move his right arm. With intensive physical therapy and the passage of time, Frank was able to regain his speech and most of his arm function. But he went into a severe "post-stroke depression" that required antidepressant treatment. The medication helped quite a bit with Frank's energy level, appetite, and sleep—but Frank continued to brood about his situation. "Why *me*?" he would ask his daughter. "I've always lived a good, honest life. I have friends older than me, and *they* don't have strokes. It's just not fair. Sometimes I feel like I'm out on some desert island, and nobody can find me."

It's certainly understandable that Frank—or anybody—would feel sad or demoralized, at times, after a serious stroke. In many cases, depression following a stroke may be due to actual damage to pathways in the brain that influence mood. But in Frank's case, something more may be going on. People who become depressed often express feelings of being "singled out," "all alone," or, in some way, feeling that life has been terribly unfair to them. And, of course, sometimes it has! In Frank's case, suffering a stroke seemed like getting struck by a bolt of lightening. There was nothing in his experience that could have prepared him for this terrible event.

35

But from the Stoic perspective, Frank has not yet been able to appreciate some very basic truths about the way life works—and about how the universe is structured. Nothing has happened to Frank that hasn't happened to men and women in their 70s for thousands of years (though our ancestors rarely lived long enough to have a stroke at such a ripe old age). Most likely, despite all our medical advances, people will continue to suffer strokes—or cancer, heart attacks, and serious accidents—for many years to come. *This is the way things are*—and Frank's sense of being singled out, or out on "a desert island," arises from an incomplete picture of reality. This emphatically does *not* mean that Frank's feelings are *wrong*, or that they shouldn't be respected! Feelings are just feelings—they aren't right or wrong. But it does mean that we can help Frank by helping him to see that nothing has befallen him that is not "conformable to the nature of the universe." This might involve, for example, putting Frank in touch with other men his age who have experienced a stroke and managed to "bounce back." Frank's psychiatrist wound up recommending that Frank volunteer twice a week at a local hospital, wheeling severely ill patients down to various appointments. When Frank was able to see people in much worse shape than himself—as well as to contribute something positive to their lives—he began to see his own problems in a broader perspective.

~

Sorrows, Beauty, and Meaning

The psychotherapist and former Catholic monk, Thomas Moore, has a valuable perspective on the role of suffering in human life:

> *Sorrow removes your attention from the active life and focuses it on the things that matter most. When you are going through a period of extreme loss or pain, you reflect on the people who mean the most to you instead of on personal success; and the deep design of your life, instead of distracting gadgets and entertainments. You may be more open to the beauty of your world as a relief from distress. Beauty is always present, but ordinarily you may not notice it because of your priorities or your absorption in other things. (*Dark Nights of the Soul, 211*)*

~

Resent a thing by all means if it represents an injustice decreed against yourself personally; but if this same constraint is binding on the lowest and the highest alike, then make your peace again with destiny.
—Seneca, Letter XCI (Campbell, 182)

Shortly after her 38th birthday, Celia—a busy administrator at an HMO—found herself feeling tired, weak, and "just plain sick as a dog." Despite several examinations by physicians, nobody could pinpoint the cause of Celia's complaints. Then, after she experienced swelling and pain in her wrists and knees, further testing revealed that Celia had *rheumatoid arthritis*, a multi-system inflammatory disease of unknown origin. Celia took the news badly. She became quite angry with her doctors for "not nipping this thing in the bud," although she was told by a rheumatologist that there was no way the disease could have been prevented. Celia withdrew from her friends and colleagues, and began to see herself as "cursed." She complained to her sister, "I don't know what I did to deserve this. They tell me it's a lifelong illness and there's no cure. I don't have time for this crap!" Celia's rheumatologist tried to be supportive, but to no avail. Celia seemed enraged with him, with her life, and with her fate. Finally, her doctor invited Celia to meet with a young woman named Samantha—who, at age 16, had been diagnosed with the *juvenile* form of the disease and had been struggling with it for several years. Despite her youth and great misfortune, Samantha maintained a hopeful attitude. She told Celia, "Yeah, it kinda sucks, but worse things happen to people. I just try to live each day the best I can."

Gradually, Celia began to move away from her position of anger and resentment. She took a part-time job volunteering in the pediatrics unit at her local hospital, and eventually came to accept her condition with greater equanimity.

Disease, disability, and ultimately death are, indeed, constraints "binding on the lowest and the highest alike." We can resent this reality, or we can get on with life. Seneca imagines Nature saying to us, "Those things you grumble about are the same for everyone. I can give no one anything any easier. But anyone who likes may make them easier for himself. How? By viewing them with equanimity" (Letter XCI, Campbell, 182–3).

As Rabbi Rami Shapiro puts it:

Life is tough, and there is a natural suffering that comes with that . . . But why add to that natural suffering with the unnecessary suffering that arises when we refuse to let go when there is no way we can hold on? . . . Don't take life so seriously. It's only temporary. We are all too serious, casting our most ordinary lives as extraordinary dramas. . . . The extent to which we get trapped in this theater is the extent to which we miss out on real life. . . . [So] get involved. We are life's way of getting things done. (Shapiro, in Olitzky & Forman, 234–5)

∽

Why be unhappy about something if it can be fixed? If it cannot be fixed, what does being unhappy help?

—*Shantideva*

In his book, Infinite Life, *Robert Thurman draws frequently from the writings of Shantideva, an eighth-century Indian monk and one of the most renowned figures in Mahayana Buddhism. Although the Buddhist tradition is quite distinct from that of Greco-Roman stoicism, the two systems have many elements in common. One error is to suppose that either tradition encourages us to be "doormats"—to accept passively whatever evil befalls us. On the contrary, Thurman tells us, "Don't think that the spiritual thing to do is to swallow your feelings and be a victim. Not at all. The point is not to allow injustice . . . to flourish. Doing nothing could not be more wrong. When something unjust happens, step in at once. Develop the ability to act forcefully without getting angry . . . Get help. Be assertive. Cheerful aggressiveness is the ticket here" (Thurman, 169–70). This doctrine is similar to that of the Jewish mystics who gathered around Moses Cordovero (1522–1570) in the village of Safed. Among their beliefs were "forbearance in the face of insult" and "complete absence of anger." However, the latter was to be "combined with* appropriate action*" (Besserman, 74–5, emphasis mine). To put it in the modern parlance of Ellis and Harper, if Joe is behaving badly toward me, the question for me is, "How can I calmly and effectively induce Joe not to act badly again?" (Ellis & Harper, 105).*

Seneca on Wisdom

For Seneca, insofar as we can ever attain wisdom, it is by "learning not to aggravate the world's obstinacy through our own responses, through spasms of rage, self-pity, anxiety, bitterness, self-righteousness and paranoia. . . . Philosophy must reconcile us to the true dimensions of reality, and so spare us, if not frustration itself, then at least its panoply of pernicious accompanying emotions." (de Botton, 81)

∼

The *Sukkah* is designed to warn us that man is not to put his trust in the size or strength or beauty of his home, though it be filled with all precious things; nor must he rely upon the help of any human being, however powerful. But let him put his trust in the great God whose word called the universe into being.
—Isaac Aboab, *Menorat Hama'or III* 4:6 (Ed. Mossad Harav Kook, 315).

The non-Jewish (and non-religious) reader will most likely need a little assistance here—and may well be wondering what all this has to do with Stoicism. So, to back up a bit: Rabbi Isaac Aboab de Fonseca (1605–1693), one of the great ethicists of the Middle Ages, was discussing the Jewish holiday of Sukkot, which falls shortly after the better-known holidays of Rosh ha-Shana and Yom Kippur. During Sukkot, Jews are commanded to erect a booth (called a *sukkah*) large enough for a family to live in. These temporary dwellings represent the tents in which the Jewish people lived during their forty years of wandering in the desert. To put Rabbi Aboab's point in more modern terms, we can cite the words of Rabbi Irving Greenberg, who tells us, "The *sukkah* provides a corrective to the natural tendency of becoming excessively attached to turf" (in Telushkin 1991, 572). In the larger sense, "turf" refers to all those material comforts that provide us with a sense of safety, security, and often prestige. (We often speak of "turf wars" between competing corporations or business moguls—suggesting, perhaps, the shallowness of this preoccupation.) In the aftermath of Hurricane Katrina, in which thousands of homes were swept away, Rabbi Aboab's comment reminds us that such dwellings are neither permanent nor trustworthy. Nor should such edifices become the focus of our inner lives. As Rabbi Shari Shamah puts it, "The house itself doesn't matter; rather, it's the people inside the house . . . and the greater community in which [the houses] dwell" (www.congshalom.org/shamahmsg.shtml).

So—how does all this fit in with the Stoic worldview? The Stoics distinguish time and again between those things that are within our power or control and those that are not. Epictetus tells us, "Within our power are the Will, and all voluntary actions; out of our power are the body and its parts, property, relatives, country, and in short, all our fellow beings" (Bonforte, 22). Later, He reminds us, "If you fulfill your duties, you have what belongs to you. For it is not the business of a philosopher to take care of mere externals—his wine, his oil, his body—but of his Reason" (73).

Putting the views of Rabbi Aboab and Epictetus together, and writing in a more modern idiom, we might produce something like this: "Look, you can put all your faith in external objects, or the opinions of others, or in the beauty of your body—but you will be fooling yourself and setting yourself up for a real 'crash.' You have no real control over these things. Houses are swept away in floods; opinions come and go; beauty is painfully transient. So in what should you invest your trust? Where should you place your best energies? Well—you should invest your trust in the Eternal. You can call this by the name of 'God' or 'Nature' or 'Logos'—or you can think of it as the underlying natural structure of the Universe. You can think of it as simply, 'The Way Things Are.' And you are privileged to be a small piece of this Great Order, insofar as you exercise the faculty that makes you truly human—*your reason*. And when you do so exercise your reason, and put yourself in harmony with The Way Things Are, you will realize that you are put here, in this world, to carry out your responsibilities as a human being—to be moral, decent, kind, and fair. And if you succeed in that, you possess not only all that you need, but all that ever really belonged to you."

~

Seneca on Fortune

> *[The wise] will start each day with the thought . . . Fortune gives us nothing which we can really own. Nothing, whether public or private, is stable; the destinies of men, no less than those of cities, are in a whirl. Whatever structure has been reared by a long sequence of years . . . is scattered and dispersed in a single day. No, he who has said "a day" has granted too long a postponement to swift misfortune; an hour, an instant of time, suffices for the overthrow of empires. (de Botton, 91)*

The Way Things Are

When a family member of mine became seriously ill, I needed to make many trips over great distances in order to help take care of him. Owing to the nature of his illness, it was nearly impossible to predict when I might be needed, when I would have to cancel professional or family plans, etc. I often found myself ruminating on the stark uncertainty of my situation, and feeling quite anxious about "when the other shoe would drop." It was also easy to feel pangs of self-pity from time to time.

But the quote from Marcus Aurelius—"Nothing will happen to me which is not conformable to the nature of the universe"—was a source of great solace and serenity. When people face uncertain and anxiety-provoking situations, they sometimes feel as if nobody else in the world is going through—or has ever gone through!—the kind of stress they are experiencing. Of course, tens of thousands—perhaps millions—have probably gone through something quite similar for millennia. People get sick; their families are called upon to comfort and care for them—and people die, often leaving others behind to grieve. These matters are not easy or pleasant—but as Marcus knew, there is really nothing bizarre or out of the ordinary in them. This is the way things are—this is our life as vulnerable and mortal creatures. Our sorrows and travails are nothing the universe has not seen many times before, and will see countless times again. And somehow—for me, anyway—this is comforting.

Chapter Seven

Living in the Here and Now

Leave the past to itself, entrust the future to providence, and content your-self with bringing holiness and justice to the present.

—Marcus Aurelius, *Meditations*
(modified slightly from Long, Book XII, Chap. 1)

Joe, a 45-year-old married engineer, was someone who never lived in the present. When he wasn't crucifying himself for some perceived "sin" or shortcoming, he was imagining new ways in which things might "go wrong." While trying to care for his terminally ill father, Joe castigated himself for "not being a better son," and worried incessantly about "how I'm going to take care of Dad when he gets closer to death." For example, Joe ruminated constantly about his father's "living will," and exactly what each stipulation meant. As a result of always looking backward or forward, Joe rarely had a moment's peace when actually spending time with his father. At one point, his father commented, "You know, Joe, it would be great to just spend some time watching a ball game with you, instead of dealing with what was, or what might be."

There's a sadly amusing cartoon by Bunny Hoest and John Reiner (*Parade Magazine*, 2/27/05) that shows a rather perturbed gentleman standing in front of a greeting card display. He inquires of the clerk: "Do you have a card that says, 'I'm sorry for everything in the past, present, and future?'"

One of the great liberating ideas of Stoic philosophy is the concept of "present contentment." In effect, the Stoic says, "I can't change the past; I can't really determine or control the future; so the best I can do is live a life of decency and integrity—*right here, right now.*" Similarly, the renowned physician, William Osler, once counseled, "Sufficient to the day is the good thereof." Marcus adds, "Let not the future trouble you; for you will come to it, if come you must, bearing with you the same reason which you are using now to meet the present" (Farquharson, 44).

What does Marcus mean by "bearing with you the same reason which you are using now to meet the present"? I believe he is saying, "Trust yourself to be a person of strength and reason, just as you are this very moment." Of course, you might reply, "But at this very moment, I'm a complete basket case!" Well, maybe so. But most people can point to many difficult situations they have faced, and faced down—whether the loss of a loved one, handling the breakup of a relationship, or dealing with a painful physical problem. It's helpful, in fact, to look back on such examples of one's self-mastery and to say, in effect, "If I could handle all that, I can handle whatever comes down the road." And for now—your responsibility is simply to "do the right thing": to bring "holiness and justice" to the present. As Rabbi Nachman of Breslov cautions us, "Yesterday and tomorrow are humanity's downfall. Today you may be aroused toward God. But yesterday and tomorrow pull you back" (Olitzky and Forman, 178).

∼

Letting Go of the Day's Woes

Finish each day and be done with it. You have done what you could; some blunders and absurdities have crept in; forget them as soon as you can. Tomorrow is a new day; you shall begin it serenely and with too high a spirit to be encumbered with your old nonsense."

—*Ralph Waldo Emerson (*The American Scholar)

∼

What remains except to enjoy life, joining one good thing to another, so as to leave not even the smallest interval unfilled?

—Marcus Aurelius (Farquharson, 92)

Brandon's big complaint was with "how little time I have to do the things I enjoy." A computer programmer who yearned to be a poet, Brandon used to fume while standing in line at the bank or the grocery: this was "just one more example of how my time is being eaten away." Brandon lived alone, and would sometimes spend hours reading the newspapers. He rationalized this by arguing, "I have to keep up with what's going on in the world." Yet he allowed himself very little time to work on his poetry. When a friend confronted him on this point, Brandon replied rather testily, "You can't just do poetry in dribs and drabs! You have to have a few hours spread out before you, like a giant canvas."

The great sages of the Stoic, Judaic, and Eastern traditions knew that Brandon's view of time is a self-injurious dodge. Marcus urges us to leave not even the smallest interval unfilled—and we might add, "or un*fulfilled*." He goes on to observe, "What a fraction of infinite and gaping time has been assigned to every man; for very swiftly it vanishes in the eternal . . ." (Farquharson, 93). But what little time we have may still be put to good use, if we set our mind upon it. After all, Brandon could be jotting down words or poetic images while standing in line at the bank—or at least reading a book of poetry. And as for the "giant canvas" of time, this, too, is a cop-out. Rabbi Menachem Mendel Schneerson—the founder of the Lubavitcher movement—used to say, "In five minutes, so much can be accomplished." Similarly, the great sage Hillel tells us, "Do not say 'When I have leisure I will study,' for you may never have leisure" (Pirke Avot 2:5). No—life is such that we must use every spare minute to accomplish our goals. The Chinese scholar, Chu Hsi, tells us, "In making the effort, a student mustn't say that he's waiting to make one big effort. He should accumulate fragments [of effort] little by little starting immediately. Waiting just to make the big effort is to waste the opportunities before him at the moment" (Gardner, 102).

By the way, the quotation from Marcus Aurelius seems to be one of the rare instances in which a Stoic philosopher explicitly urges us to "enjoy life!" And yet, one can see the whole of Marcus's philosophy as an attempt to create a rich, meaningful, and purposive existence. To achieve this, however, we must constantly ask, "How is the governing self employing itself?" How well are we using our precious time? "For therein," Marcus notes, "is everything" (Farquharson, 93).

~

A Buddhist View of Staying in the Moment

> *Do not pursue the past. Do not lose yourself in the future. The past no longer is. The future has not yet come. Looking deeply at life as it is, in the very here and now, the practitioner dwells in stability and freedom.*
>> —From the Bhaddekaratta Sutta, *as translated by Thich Nhat Hanh*
>> *(in Kornfield, 118–19)*

Do Not "Kill Time"

Rabbi Kerry N. Olitzky tells us,

> *While we often take time for granted, it is probably the most precious commodity available to us. To "kill time," therefore, is particularly nefarious. Some of*

us naively refuse to acknowledge the passing of time, specifically when it comes to marking the years of our life as we get older. Others, however, thankful for those years and the life that has been granted to them . . . enthusiastically welcome these birthdays . . . Enjoy the day ahead and treasure each moment." (Olitzky & Forman, 1999)

In her book, A Sideways Look at Time, *Jay Griffiths reminds us that we can also become* prisoners *of time. Interestingly, she cites Seneca as asking, "When shall we live, if not now?" This reminds us of Hillel's famous question: "If I am not for myself, who will be for me? And if I am for myself alone, what am I? And if not now, when?" Griffiths also cites the* Tao Te Ching *as teaching us, "Move with the present." The underlying idea in all these traditions is that—while we should not waste time—neither should we be slaves to it, by being mired in the past, or obsessively focused on the future. As Nachman of Bratslav tells us, "For all man has in the world is the day and the hour where he is; for the morrow is an entirely different world.*

Time and the Art of Happiness

Rabbi Joseph Telushkin (2006, 63) writes that, to use time well, we must avoid telling ourselves two things:

- *"I have plenty of time." If we do, then it means that there is something empty or missing in our lives.*
- *"I have no time at all." This often becomes a rationale for not doing things that we can do.*

~

Do not dwell upon all the manifold troubles which have come to pass and will come to pass, but ask yourself in regard to every present piece of work: what is there here that can't be borne and can't be endured?

—Marcus Aurelius (Farquharson, 57).

Lori was a 27-year old business manager in a large biotechnology firm. She had been very successful in her work, until a new supervisor was assigned to her department. Almost immediately, Lori began to feel her spirits sink. "This guy is constantly criticizing me," she complained. "Everything I do, he has something bad to say about it. Not only that, he's telling me I have to increase my "efficiency" or face a possible layoff." Lori began to go into "an emotional tailspin," imagining herself unemployed and "out on the street." She also began to doubt her own competence as a manager, wondering how she would ever be able to deal with any management jobs in the future. Her sleep and appetite began to suffer, and Lori found herself "downing a couple of cocktails each night, just to fall asleep." A co-worker suggested that Lori talk to the company's psychologist.

It's very likely that Lori's psychologist gave her advice along the lines of Marcus Aurelius's: focus on the here and now; ask yourself what it is about the present situation that is so unbearable; and don't turn one setback into a cosmic disaster that will ruin every other aspect of your life. After all, even if Lori were to lose her job, who's to say she couldn't find another one and be quite happy with it? And, as Ellis and Harper point out, "Upsetting yourself about other people and events will usually sidetrack you from what should logically be your main concern: the way *you* behave, the things *you* do" (Ellis & Harper, 164). Maybe Lori's supervisor isn't just an obnoxious jerk — maybe some of his criticisms have merit. Lori might well decide that the best course is a "proactive" one, in which she seeks a meeting with her supervisor, in order to solicit more constructive feedback and to express a willingness to modify her approach. If this fails to correct the situation, Lori might well consider asking for a transfer within the company, or seeking another job. Falling into an "emotional tailspin" is certainly not our only option when faced with life's "manifold troubles."

~

What's the Worst that Can Happen?

As Alain de Botton observes, sometimes "reassurance can be the cruelest antidote to anxiety. Our rosy predictions both leave the anxious unprepared for the worst, and unwittingly imply that it would be disastrous if the worst came to pass. Seneca more wisely asks us to consider that bad things probably will occur, but adds that they are unlikely ever to be as bad as we fear" (de Botton, 96). Indeed, Seneca counsels us, "If you wish to put off all worry, assume that what you fear may happen is certainly going to happen." As de Botton notes, "Seneca wagered that once we look rationally at what will occur if our desires are not fulfilled, we almost certainly find that the underlying problems are more modest than the anxieties they have bred" (de Botton, 97). Or, as Drs. Albert Ellis and Robert Harper put it, "The assumed catastrophic quality of most potentially unpleasant events is almost invariably highly exaggerated. . . . the worst thing about almost any "disaster" is usually your exaggerated belief in its horror, rather than anything intrinsically terrible about it" (Ellis & Harper, 133).

Chapter Eight

The Opinion of Others

You say, people cannot admire the sharpness of your wits—be it so: but . . .
[you can] show those qualities which are altogether in your power: sincerity,
gravity, endurance of labor . . . contentment with your portion and with few
things, benevolence, [and] frankness.

—Marcus Aurelius, *Meditations* (Long, 80–81)

Bryce was an aspiring novelist who found himself stuck in a "dead end" job
as a junior executive at an insurance company. No matter how many innova-
tive ideas Bryce came up with, his boss would always pour cold water on
them. "He just blows me off," Bryce told his therapist, "even when he knows
my ideas are good, and would save the company money." To deal with his
frustrations, Bryce would write short stories. But though he enjoyed writing,
the frequent rejections by many literary journals left Bryce bitter and resentful. "I can't believe the junk these guys publish!" he complained. "But when
I send them something really good, they reject it with some stupid form letter. And you wonder why I'm upset!" Bryce had become so frustrated with
his work and his writing that, lately, he had started to abuse alcohol.

The Stoics would have a good deal to say to Bryce, who has come to see
himself as a poor victim of ungrateful bosses and unappreciative editors. Fun-
damentally, Bryce wants something that nobody can have: *control over how
others feel about our work, talent, and value.* As Ellis and Harper might say
to Bryce, "There's only one possible thoroughgoing solution to your problem.
And that is, of course, that you give up the idea that you must be approved or
loved by others in order to deem yourself worthwhile in your own right" (83).

But Marcus Aurelius goes beyond noting that we must accept the fact that
our "sharp wits" often go unappreciated. He tells us to focus on what we *can*

46

control: *our own attitude and behavior.* Nobody can prevent us from acting with kindness, integrity, or gratitude. Nobody can prevent us from being content with the cards life has dealt us. True—we can't always behave or think in such an exemplary manner, but with effort, we can do so much of the time. The Chinese sage, Confucius, put it this way: "A wise man is not distressed that people do not know him; he is distressed at his own lack of ability" (Dover, 87).

If Bryce were to take this to heart, he would have nothing to fear from either his boss or those insensitive editors.

~

Which of these is lovely because it is praised, or corrupted because it is blamed? Does an emerald become worse than it was, if it be not praised? And what of gold, ivory, purple, a lute . . . a flower bud . . . ?
—*Marcus Aurelius (Farquharson, 21)*

~

Will any man despise me? Let him see to it. But I will see to it that I may not be found doing or saying anything that deserves to be despised.
—Marcus Aurelius (Farquharson, 82).

Ray was not popular in his small, rural congregation. Although a devout "believer," Ray felt that his minister had "gone way too far" in bringing politics into his weekly sermons. According to Ray, "Rev. Thomas keeps bringing in all these right-wing ideas he takes from some of our worst demagogues and politicians. I've spoken to him about it, but he says that people of faith have to be political, and that I should just keep quiet." A number of people in Ray's congregation had started spreading rumors about him—that Ray was "a bleeding-heart liberal," that he "wanted to turn the Church over to the abortionists," and so on. At first, Ray became quite angry when he learned of this malicious gossip, and resolved to "publicly denounce" those he suspected of spreading these statements. However, his wife suggested that Ray take the likely offenders aside and speak to them calmly and gently about his concerns. "Listen, Hon," she added, "we just have to tend our own gardens."

When we are attacked, our natural instinct is to strike back in some way. I'm not speaking now of legitimate self-defense, but of the tendency to react angrily when we are criticized or maligned. Certainly, being the object of malicious gossip is not pleasant. But Marcus teaches us that the best strategy is often to say of these gossips, "That's their problem. I need to make sure— through my own behavior—that there is no basis for their slander." Thomas a Kempis expresses a similar thought when he says, "Firstly, be peaceful yourself, and you will be able to bring peace to others" (70–71). Similarly, the *Talmud* reminds us, "Those who are besieged by anger have no life" (Pesahim 1123b).

w

~

Watch Your Words

> *The person who guards his speech builds real power. This is the power of self-discipline, the knowledge that one has control over his impulses; that he has the inner strength to restrain himself, measure his words, and act in accordance with the highest aspects of himself.*
> *—Chofetz Chaim (*Yisrael Meier Kagan, ca. 1870; cited in
> Finkelman & Berkowitz 1995, xxxviii)*

Pride of Place?

Seneca reminds us of our tendency to over-react when we feel that we have been insulted or slighted:

> *Because you are given a less honorable place at the table, you begin to get angry at your host . . . [and] at the man himself who was preferred above you. Madman! What difference does it make on what part of the couch you recline? Can a cushion add either to your honor or your disgrace?* (On Anger, *cited in Telushkin 2006, 233)*

Telushkin goes on to remind us that, "Many of us go through life as 'bad guests,' minimizing the good others have done for us . . . if someone has done us a favor, we should focus on the good done, not on the fact that the person could have done more" (2006, 106).

Chapter Nine

The Common Bond of Being

All things are woven together and the common bond is sacred . . . for there is one Universe out of all, one God through all, one substance and one law, one common Reason of all intelligent creatures, and one truth . . .
— Marcus Aurelius (Farquharson, 45)

Mitch was a 29-year-old, single accountant living in Manhattan. After the attacks of 9/11, Mitch couldn't sleep for a month. He had been working just three blocks from the Twin Towers when they fell, and he lost two close friends. Although he recovered his usual sleep patterns after another two months, Mitch was left with a brooding hatred of what he called, "the f—-ing Towel Heads who did this to my friends." Mitch began to withdraw from his family and co-workers, entering what he described as " . . . sort of a dark tunnel. I would just lie around in bed, not shower or shave, and go through all these revenge scenarios. You know, how to get back at the S.O.B.s who did this."

Mitch's feelings after 9/11 were probably shared, to varying degrees, by millions of Americans. And let's be clear—the actions of the terrorists were cowardly, despicable, and unconscionable. Such *behavior* is worthy of our hatred—and yet, we must make an effort to avoid hating *our fellow human beings*. This may be nearly impossible for most of us, when it comes to the very worst of the lot—the bin Ladens, Hitlers, Pol Pots, and Stalins of the world. *And yet, and yet*—the Stoic message is that we must at least try! Marcus tells us, "The best way of avenging yourself is not to become like the wrongdoer" (Long, 105).

In the Judaic tradition, too, this teaching is emphasized. In the *Talmud*, we are told, "A bad eye, bad passion, and hatred of one's fellow creatures drive a person out of the world" (Pirkei Avot 2:16). Rabbi Moshe Lieber notes that

" . . . we must treat people properly because all people play a role in God's plans; nobody was created for naught, be it a fool, an ignoramus, or even an evil person. They are all part of the Divine scheme. We may not understand how this can be, but God created everything and everyone so that something good and beneficial will come from each of them" (1995, 222).

This sentiment is not far from the Stoic claim that "All things are woven together and the common bond is sacred."

∿

Seneca, On Hatred

Hatred is not only a vice, but a vice which goes point-blank against Nature.
Hatred divides instead of joining and frustrates God's will in human society.
One man is born to help another.
Hatred makes us destroy one another.
Love unites—hatred separates.
Love is beneficial—hatred is destructive.
Love succors even strangers—hatred destroys the most intimate friendship.
Love fills all hearts with joy—hatred ruins all those who possess it.
Nature is bountiful—hatred is pernicious.
It is not hatred, but mutual love, that holds all mankind together. (cited in Davis 1903)

∿

We are here for this—to make mistakes and to correct ourselves, to stand the blows and hand them out. We must never feel disarmed: nature is immense and complex, but it is not impermeable to the intelligence; we must circle around it, pierce and probe it, look for the opening or make it.
                                        —Primo Levi (from *The Periodic Table*)

The author and Holocaust survivor Primo Levi speaks to the "tragic predicament" of human life, and how we must strive to surmount it. This was brought home to me in a recent exchange with Leonard Rosen, a professor at Bentley College. Prof. Rosen described his sudden bout with Bell's Palsy, a neurological disorder that causes temporary paralysis of the facial muscles. From his frightening experience, Rosen drew a number of important lessons relevant to both Stoic and existential philosophy:

On the first day of spring this year, I awoke to find that only half of my face could smile. The other half drooped . . . no matter how hard I tried to rescue it. . . . For the moment, I'll have to be agnostic on the advice I heard years ago: that each day we must decide if life is comic or tragic and then live accordingly. My question-mark face suggests that life must be both . . . A resolution, then, for the day my smile returns: to place on my already cluttered desk a replica of the ancient masks . . . one side, eyes crinkled with joy; the other, raising a wail to heaven. I may never understand the balance of fortune and misfortune in the world, but what I do with that reminder, each day, will be the measure of my worth. (*Boston Globe*, 3/24/06)

Chapter Ten

Character and Happiness

To straighten the crooked, you must first do a harder thing—straighten yourself. You are your only master. Who else? Subdue yourself, and discover your master.

—from the *Dhammapada* (in Kornfield, 65)

Irwin and Ruth, a successful couple in their 60s, decided they needed to "spice up" their marriage with a big splurge: a get-away trip to Hawaii. After 35 years of marriage, Ruth described things at home as " . . . just kind of boring. Irwin is a wonderful guy, but we never really do anything. All he wants to do is sit and read. Me, I like to go out and dance!" Irwin's response was one of slightly wounded puzzlement: "I love Ruth. I don't know what she's complaining about. I mean, we go out to dinner twice a week! On my salary, that's pretty good. I just wish Ruth would stop *noodging* me all the time." When the trip finally got underway, both Ruth and Irwin found that Hawaii " . . . didn't do much to change things for us." Although she enjoyed Hawaii's beauty, Ruth still found that Irwin wanted to spend most of his time " . . . lounging around the hotel pool, like a stick in the mud, and guess what? Reading!" Irwin complained that, ". . . the whole time, all I heard from her was, 'Let's go explore the volcano! Let's take a sail boat out to one of the other islands!' I don't know why she can't just enjoy relaxing."

One of the myths our culture likes to propagate is that of the "Magical Vacation"—the perfect cruise or island getaway that "will make you forget your cares and give you back your zest for life!" Seneca and the Stoics knew better—they understood that when travel is approached in this way, it is truly a Fool's Paradise. As Seneca tells us in his letters, "Whatever your destination, you will be followed by your failings." He quotes Socrates as saying to a disappointed voyager, "How can you wonder your travels do you no good, when you carry yourself around with you? You are saddled with the very thing that drove you away" (Campbell, 75). And, ultimately, he sums this position up by saying, "A change of character, not a change of air, is what you need" (Letter XXVIII, Campbell, 75).

This doesn't mean we shouldn't take vacations with an attitude of hope and enthusiasm—but we also need to be realistic. When the cruise ship docks at the home port, we are back to our old problems, and our old selves. And what will we do with those "saddlebags"? Seneca has a ready answer: "What you must do, then, is mend your ways and get rid of the burden you're carrying. Keep your cravings within safe limits. Scour every trace of evil from your personality. If you want to enjoy your travel, you must make your traveling companion a healthy one" (Campbell, 190).

~

A good character is the only guarantee of everlasting, carefree happiness.

—Seneca, Letter XXVII (Campbell, 73)

Jim was a 60-year-old city councilman with a distinguished record in his community. He had served faithfully in city government for over thirty years and had a reputation for honesty and integrity. Jim and his family, however, had to make do on a very modest salary, and were under enormous financial pressure, owing to his wife's chronic medical problems. One day, Jim was approached by an individual who identified himself as a member of a "political action committee." This person related a convoluted story about " . . . how badly our group needs your help, Jim," which culminated in an offer to pay Jim $50,000 if he would vote in favor of a certain proposal coming before the town council. To his surprise, Jim actually considered the offer for a moment, before turning it down and ejecting the malefactor from his office.

The Stoics knew the value of good character, just as the rabbis of the *Talmud* did. In Pirke Avot, Rabbi Shimon says: "There are three crowns: the crown of *Torah*, the crown of priesthood, and the crown of royalty, but the crown of a good name is superimposed on them all" (4:17). Fair enough—but in what sense is a good character the guarantor of "everlasting, carefree happiness"? Surely, even if our habitual ethical behavior gives us some sense of satisfaction, there is nothing "everlasting" in this, nor a guarantee that we shall feel "carefree!" The Stoics beg to differ. To understand their reasoning, we must begin with the Stoic's premise that the only thing in life we can even hope to control is our *own attitude*—and, derivatively, our response to life's "slings and arrows." This *inner conviction* is not something that can be taken from us, as a thief might take our money. And, the Stoics argue, insofar as we commit ourselves to acting in harmony with the Universe or Logos—accepting the way things are and striving to harm no one—we hitch our star to something everlasting. Moreover, when we feel ourselves in harmony with universal nature and mankind, *we experience a deep and enduring sense of happiness*. Seneca adds, "We have neither successes nor setbacks as individuals; our lives have a common end. No one can lead a happy life if he thinks only of himself and turns everything to his own purpose" (Campbell, 96). On some level, Jim must have known this.

∾

To Thine Own Self Be True?

Before he died, Rabbi Zusya said: "In the world to come they will not ask me, 'Why were you not Moses?' They will ask me, 'Why were you not Zusya?'" (Attributed to Hasidic Rabbi Zusya of Hanipoli).

The Stoic tradition also places great importance on being true to oneself—but not in the narcissistic sense, popularized in the '60s, of "doing your own thing." Rather, the Stoics have in mind identifying and fulfilling *one's true nature. Marcus Aurelius tells us that "those who do not observe the movements of their own minds must of necessity be unhappy" (Long, 23). He also notes, "Nothing is more wretched than the man who goes round and round everything . . . and seeks by conjecture to sound the minds of his neighbors, but fails to perceive that it is enough to abide with the Divinity that is within himself" (Farquharson, 10). Rabbi Zusya needed to be Rabbi Zusya—not Moses!*

∾

Take heed not to be transformed into a Caesar . . . Keep yourself therefore simple, good, pure, grave, unaffected, the friend of justice, religious, kind, affectionate, strong for your proper work. Wrestle to continue to be the [kind of person] Philosophy wished to make you.
—Marcus Aurelius, *Meditations* (Farquharson, 39)

Heather was what her co-workers in the corporate world called "a real go-getter." At the age of only 32, she was already Vice President of Marketing at a large pharmaceutical firm. As a single woman with a fierce devotion to her work, Heather was also known as a "workaholic." She would sometimes spend 16 hours a day at the office, and slog home with work still in hand. Unfortunately, as she moved up the corporate ladder, Heather became increasingly attracted to the trappings of power. She bought herself a penthouse condo in the fanciest part of town. She spent a fortune on clothes, cosmetics, and lavish parties for her colleagues. And yet, Heather had few friends, or even sympathetic co-workers. Most of those who worked under her found Heather haughty and overbearing. She once humiliated a trainee in front of his peers, after he made a minor error, and then refused to apologize for her behavior. Heather's mantra at work was, "You have a choice: be a live shark or a dead guppy." Eventually, Heather was reprimanded by her boss for being verbally abusive to a subordinate, and was transferred to a lower-echelon position.

I alluded earlier to the Judaic concept of *heshbon ha-nefesh*—roughly, "accounting of the soul." Marcus hints at this in urging that we "take heed" to avoid the arrogance and lust for power that characterized Julius Caesar, and that we "wrestle" with ourselves for our own betterment. Marcus then gives us a brief checklist of moral qualities that we must seek to preserve in ourselves—a list Heather would have done well to examine.

Rabbi Goldie Milgram expands on the idea of a moral inventory, and on the construct of *heshbon ha-nefesh* as originally conceived by the 19th century sage, Rabbi Mendel of Satanov. In the following list, italics identify Rabbi Mendel's items in his moral inventory; in normal font are Rabbi Milgram's commentaries (http://www.reclaimingjudaism.org/Heshbon.htm). Note, in particular, the quintessentially Stoic values of *equanimity, tolerance, humility, calmness, temperance*, and *deliberation*. Taken in toto, this inventory shows us a pathway to personal happiness and responsible living—which turn out to be much the same thing.

- *Equanimity*. Ability to live in balance.
- *Tolerance*. Growing pains lead to knowing gains.
- *Orderliness*. Allocating time for living life fully with integrity.
- *Decisiveness*. Acting promptly when your reasoning is sure.
- *Cleanliness*. Modeling dignity in your ways and space.
- *Humility*. Knowing you will always have much to learn and more opinions than answers.
- *Righteousness*. Conducting your life such that you are trusted and respected.
- *Economic Stability*. Safeguarding enough resources for yourself to live without debt.
- *Zeal*. Living with gusto focused on purpose and care.
- *Silence*. Listening and reflecting before speaking.
- *Calmness*. Giving your needs and thoughts gently while being respectful and clear.

- *Truth*. Speaking only what is fully confirmed in fact.
- *Separation*. Focus on each strand in its own time, avoid multi-tasking.
- *Temperance*. Eating and drinking for good health, not dangerous excess.
- *Deliberation*. Pause before acting, consider consequences, integrate heart and mind wisely.
- *Modest Ways*. Eschewing crude, lewd, and boastful mannerisms and practices.
- *Trust*. Living in the spirit of knowing there is abundance in the universe and you are in the flow.
- *Generosity*. Finding satisfaction in making much possible for others.

~

If it's not right, don't do it; if it is not true, don't say it.
—Marcus Aurelius, Meditations, *Book XII (Farquharson, 90)*

A great deal of complex calculation often enters into our moral reasoning. We try to "psych out" what other people expect of us, determine whether or not we can get away with some dubious activity, foresee how our action may affect our financial situation, and so on. So, too, with the veracity of our speech: we may think, "If I shade the truth just a little in what I say to her, I may be able to get away with it." Marcus provides us with a simple and direct antidote to such Machiavellian scheming. He reminds us, in a closely linked passage, to " . . . relate your action to no other end except the good of human fellowship" (90). How much happier we would be if we followed Marcus's deceptively simple dictum!

Stop Complaining and Make the World a Better Place!

Compare this statement, traditionally attributed to Rabbi Abraham Isaac Kook, to Marcus Aurelius's take on the matter (following): "The pure, righteous people do not complain against wickedness but add righteousness. They do not complain against disbelief but add faith. They do not complain against ignorance but add wisdom."

> *[The magnanimous individual] . . . spends no thought about what someone may say or think about him or do against him; but [rather] is contented with these two things: if he is himself acting justly in what is done in the present; and [if] he embraces what is assigned to him in the present . . . [The magnanimous person] . . . has no other will than to pursue a straight path according to the law and . . . to follow in God's train.*
> *—Marcus Aurelius,* Meditations *(Farquaharson, 74)*

First Action, Then Holiness: The Primacy of Behavior

An admiring atheist once said to the great French scientist and mystic, Blaise Pascal (1623–62), "I wish that I had your faith, so that I might lead a life like yours." Pascal replied, "Lead my life and you will acquire my faith."

The sages of Judaism held to a similar view; i.e., that "through deed, the will is mobilized and fortified. Even if one [does] a good act out of an unworthy motive . . . he will, if he persists, come to be governed by a right motive" (Adler, 67).

Chapter Eleven

Contentment with Our Lot

Those . . . who are happy . . . have their minds fixed on some object other than their own happiness; on the happiness of others, on the improvement of mankind, even on some art or pursuit . . . aiming thus at something else, they find happiness by the way.

—John Stuart Mill

Amy and Sarah had been inseparable friends since grade school. They shared everything as teenagers—clothes, music, dating, movies, and their deepest hopes and secrets. There was nothing sexual in their relationship; Amy and Sarah were just "best friends." They applied to the same college, and went off together with every expectation that their friendship would persist. But as Sarah became more involved with Jeff—a young man in her history class— she spent less and less time with Amy, who tended to keep to herself. Amy became angry and resentful, eventually confronting Sarah and tearfully shouting, "How can you do this to me? You're a fair-weather friend and a backstabber!" It took many months before Amy could deal with the fact that, while Sarah still cared for her, Sarah had her own life to live. Eventually, Amy was able to find a new circle of friends, but still saw Sarah on occasion.

Seneca highlights a crucial distinction in human psychology, one that might have helped Amy: the distinction between *need* and *desire*. He writes, "This is what we mean when we say the wise man is self-content; he is so in the sense that he is *able* to do without friends, not that he *desires* to do without them." (Letter IX, Campbell, 48; emphasis mine). Our "pop" culture often blurs this distinction, with an endless barrage of song lyrics shouting, "I *need* you, baby!" and "Can't live without your love!", etc. Psychologist Albert Ellis has been in the forefront of the movement to challenge these cultural assumptions, and would undoubtedly agree with Seneca that the fully-realized person *wants*, but does not *need,* friendship. Indeed, the cornerstone of Stoic philosophy is that before we can truly *be* a friend—and before we can *love*—we must first achieve *self-love* and *self-sufficiency.* Seneca tells us, in the same letter (IX), "Anyone thinking of his own interests and seeking out friendship with this in view is making a great mistake" (Campbell, 49). He adds, "If you wish to be loved, love." Seneca means that friendship should not aim at gaining us emotional or psychological "goods," much less material advantage. Amy's petulant reaction to Sarah's relationship with Jeff—while quite understandable—suggests that Amy was "using" Sarah to satisfy some inner need, rather than simply enjoying Sarah's companionship for its own sake. The true friend sees her companion not as an extension of her own needs, but as the recipient of her finest instincts and most generous wishes. "What is my object in making a friend?" Seneca asks. "To have someone to be able to die for, someone I may follow into exile, someone for whose life I may put myself up as security" (49).

This last image may be a subtle restatement of the famous Greek myth involving Damon and Pythias (or Phintias). In brief, Dionysius—the tyrannical ruler of Syracuse—had condemned Pythias to death. However, the king allowed Pythias to leave to settle his affairs first, as long as Damon, Pythias's friend, agreed to stay as hostage. Damon did so. When Pythias returned as promised, Dionysius was so impressed that he let them both go.

~

Any man who does not think that what he has is more than ample is an unhappy man, even if he is the master of the whole world.

—Epicurus (Campbell, 53).

We have not devoted much attention to the Epicureans, *a philosophical school that competed with the Stoics in 4th century BCE Greece. Founded by Epicurus (341–270 BCE), this school has long been misunderstood as advocating a sort of "Eat, drink, and be merry!" attitude, if not outright debauchery. This is far from the truth. Epicurus argued merely that the proper goal in life is to secure* responsible *pleasures and avoid unnecessary pain. Intellectual pleasures were preferred over sensual ones, since the latter often create serious problems in the long run. That Epicureanism was not far removed from Stoicism is indicated by Seneca's citing Epicurus' words with evident approval (Letter IX, Campbell, 53).*

The idea that true contentment lies in being satisfied with what one has is also reflected in the Talmud. *We find, for example, this statement in Pirke Avot*

(4:1): "Who is rich? One who rejoices in one's portion." Toperoff points out that this Mishnah is not simply about being "rich," but about being happy *or contented. He cites the words of the 13th-century sage, Jacob Anatoli, who said, "If a man cannot get what he wants, he ought to want what he can get" (197). This Talmudic notion of happiness, as Toperoff points out, stresses what I have described elsewhere as the "great attribute of thankfulness" (Pies 2000, 208–9). Similarly, in the* Tao Te Ching, *we find the statement, "He who is contented is rich" (Browne, 309). Thus, the Stoic concept of happiness as a kind of* grateful self-sufficiency *resonates with a number of ancient spiritual traditions.*

On Being Grateful

Marcus Aurelius begins his Meditations with a litany of "thank you" notes. As Farquharson puts it, these comprise "a personal acknowledgment of lessons learned and good gifts received from the men and women who seemed . . . to have had the most influence on his life" (95). Marcus thanks everybody from his paternal grandfather to the gods! In this respect, Marcus is demonstrating one of the less frequently noted aspects of Stoicism—its emphasis on gratitude. *The French philosopher Andre Comte-Sponville, in his excellent book,* A Small Treatise on the Great Virtues, *has this to say about gratitude:*

> *What gratitude teaches us . . . is that there is also such a thing as joyful humility, or humble joy, humble because it knows it is not its own cause . . . and, knowing this, rejoices all the more." (135)*

Gratitude, indeed, may be the deepest wisdom. As Epicurus puts it, "The fool's life is empty of gratitude and full of fears." And when I have had a particularly frustrating day, I sometimes find this Buddhist saying helpful:

> *Let us rise up and be thankful, for if we didn't learn a lot today, at least we learned a little; and if we didn't learn a little, at least we didn't get sick; and if we got sick, at least we didn't die; so let us all be thankful.*

~

It is in no man's power to have whatever he wants; but he has it in his power not to wish for what he hasn't got, and cheerfully make the most of the things that do come his way.

—Seneca, Letter CXXIII (Campbell, 227)

Rick was known in the office as "one of the movers and shakers." At the age of only 34, he was already Vice President of Corporate Management in a large biotechnology firm. Rick's friends saw him as a man who "had it all"—a great career, a beautiful and successful wife, a gorgeous house, and a manner that always seemed to put people at ease. Yet almost nobody saw the Rick who left the office and went home at night, feeling like a "fraud" and a "flop." Rick castigated himself for "not making it to President of Corporate Management" and for "getting edged out by a guy with more guts." He looked at his twelve-room house in an exclusive suburb and thought, "I could do better than this. And I would have, too, if I had just played my cards a little smarter." At the same time, Rick yearned for an entirely different life—as a history teacher. "I could kick myself for not getting my master's degree in history," Rick confided to his therapist. "By now, I could have had my PhD, and be teaching at the college." Even in his marriage, Rick always wished for more. "I love Kathy," he said, "but in a lot of ways, she's not the woman I dreamt of marrying. . . . I always wanted somebody with an artistic streak—maybe even a poet—and Kathy is so damn practical."

Rick is one of millions of people who just can't seem to find contentment with the many wonderful things they have. There is a saying in the rabbinical literature to the effect that "People never leave this world with even half their desires fulfilled" (Ecclesiasties Rabbah 1:13). If we can take this fact to heart and live out its implications, we will probably find the happiness that has eluded Rick.

References

a Kempis, T. *The Imitation of Christ*. Trans. L. Sherley-Price. London: Penguin Classics, 1952.

——. "On Bearing With The Faults of Others." In *Counsels on the Spiritual Life*. Trans. L. Sherley-Price. London: Penguin Books, 1995.

Adler, M. *The World of the* Talmud. New York: Schocken Books, 1963.

Aurelius, M. *The Meditations of Marcus Aurelius*. Trans. G. Long. Boston: Shambhala, 1993.

——. *Marcus Aurelius: Meditations*. Trans. A.S.L. Farquharson. New York: Knopf, Everyman's Library, 1946.

Baron, J.L. (Ed.) *A Treasury of Jewish Quotations*. Northvale, NJ: Jason Aronson/B'nai B'rith, 1985.

Besserman, P. *The Way of the Jewish Mystics*. Boston: Shambhala, 1994.

Boethius. *The Consolation of Philosophy*. Trans. R. Green. Indianapolis: Bobbs-Merrill, 1962.

Bonforte, J. *The Philosophy of Epictetus*. New York: Philosophical Library, 1955.

Browne, L. *The World's Great Scriptures*. New York: Macmillan, 1961.

Bulka, R.P. *Chapters of the Sages*. Northvale, NJ: Jason Aronson, 1993.

Burtt, E.A. *The Teachings of the Compassionate Buddha*. New York: Penguin Books, 1982.

Cicero. *Selected Works*. Trans. M. Grant. New York: Penguin Books, 1971.

Comte-Sponville, A: *A Small Treatise on the Great Virtues*. New York: Owl Books, 1996.

Confucius. *The Analects*. Ed. T. Crofts, trans. W.E. Soothill. Mineola, NY: Dover, 1995.

Davis, C. *Greek and Roman Stoicism*. Boston: Herbert B. Turner and Co., 1903.

de Botton, A. *The Consolations of Philosophy*. New York: Pantheon Books, 2000.

Ellis A. & Harper, R.A. *A Guide to Rational Living*. Hollywood, CA: Wilshire Book Company, 1961.

Finkelman, S., Berkowitz, Y., & Chofetz, C. *A Lesson a Day*. New York: Mesorah Publications, 1995.

Gardner, D.K. *Chu Hsi: Learning to Be a Sage*. Berkeley: University of California Press, 1990.

Gelberman J.H. *Physician of the Soul*. Freedom, CA: Crossing Press, 2000.

Grayling, A.C. *The Reason of Things*. London: Weidenfeld & Nicolson, 2002.

Halkin, A. & Hartman, D. *Epistles of Maimonides: Crisis and Leadership*. Philadelphia: The Jewish Publication Society, 1985.

Hume, R.E. *The Thirteen Principal Upanishads*. London: Oxford University Press, 1962.

Johnson, S. *Rambler #47* (August 28, 1750).

Klagsbrun, F. *Voices of Wisdom*, Boston: David R. Godine, 1990.

Kornfield, J. *Teachings of the Buddha*. Boston: Shambhala Pocket Classics, 1993.

Lankevich, G.J. (Ed.). *Wit and Wisdom of the* Talmud. Garden City, NJ: Square One Publishers, 2002.

Lieber, M. *The Pirkei Avos Treasury: Ethics of the Fathers*. New York: Mesorah Publications, 1995.

Lindeman E.C. (Ed.). *Emerson*. New York: Pelican Books, 1947.

Marinoff, L. *Therapy for the Sane*. New York: Bloomsbury, 2003.

Mascaro, J. *The Bhagavad Gita*. London: Penguin Books, 1962.

———. *The Dhammapada*. London: Penguin Books, 1973.

Montaigne, M. *On Physiognomy,* from Essays of Montaigne, vol. 9, trans. Charles Cotton, revised by William Carew Hazlett (New York: Edwin C. Hill, 1910). Accessed at: Online Library of Liberty [oll.libertyfund.org].

Moore, T. *Dark Nights of the Soul*. New York: Gotham Books, 2004.

Olitzky, K.M. & Forman, L. *Sacred Intentions*. Woodstock, VT: Jewish Lights Publishing, 1999.

Pies, R. *The Ethics of the Sages*. Northvale, NJ, Jason Aronson, 2000.

Renard, J. *The Handy Religion Answer Book*. New York: Barnes and Noble, 2004.

Seneca. *Seneca: Letters from a Stoic*. Trans. R. Campbell. London: Penguin Books, 1969.

Sherwin, B.L. & Cohen, S.J. *Creating an Ethical Jewish Life*. Woodstock, VT: Jewish Lights Publishing, 2001.

Sorabji, R. *Platonists and Stoics on the Self*. Bath Royal Literary and Scientific Institution Proceedings, vol. 9 (Feb 24, 2005).

Tanakh. Philadephia, PA: The Jewish Publication Society, 1985.

Telushkin, J. *A Code of Jewish Ethics, Volume 1*. New York: Bell Tower, 2006.

———. *Jewish Literacy*. New York: William Morrow, 1991.

Thurman, R. *Infinite Life: Seven Virtues for Living Well*. New York: Riverhead Books, 2004.

Toperoff, S.P. *Avot*. Northvale, NJ: Jason Aronson, 1997.

Index

Adler, M. (1963), 57, 63

adversity and self-possession: Boethius on, 19, 24, 25; Genesis [32:25–33], 20; grief and, 23–24; illness and, 23; Maimonides on, 19–20; preparedness and, 21–22; Seneca on, 25; Shakespeare on, 20

anger: the Book of Proverbs on, 9, 10; Epictetus on, 5–6; Rabbi Abraham Joshua Herschel on, 6; Rabbi Joseph Telushkin on, 6; and resentment, 35–37; Seneca on, 9, 48; the *Talmud* on, 48; teachings of the Rabbis on, 9

anxiety, 45

apatheia, meaning of, x

appearances, deception of, 8–9, 16

assertiveness, 38

attachments and suffering, 13–14

Aurelius, Marcus: on the art of living, 20; birth/death dates of, ix; on the common bond of being, 49; on conformity with the nature of the universe, 35, 40; on contentment, 41, 42; on the corrupting influence of power, 54; on criticism, 46–47; on duty, 17, 18; on equanimity of spirit, x; on the fear of failing, 28, 33; on gratitude, 60; on hypocrisy, 16; on ignorance, 2; on judgment, 4; on judgment of others, 34; on moral reasoning, 56; on mortality, 11, 12, 13, 30; on our insignificance, 30; on perfection of character, x; on righteousness, 56; on self-acceptance, 31; on self-reliance, 54; on things that do not touch the soul, 1, 2; on time, 43; on utopian goals, 32

Baron, J. L. (1985), xi, 63

Beck, Dr. Aaron, x

Becker, Ernest on mortality, 11

behavior, primacy of, 57

Besseman, P. (1994), 7, 32, 63

Boethius: on adversity, 19, 25; *The Consolation of Philosophy*, [trans.] R. Green (1962), 25, 63; on good fortune, 24; on self-possession, 19

Bonforte, J. (1955), 18, 63, 92

the Book of Proverbs [15:32] on understanding, 30

The Boston Globe, an article on fear of failure, 28

Browne, L. (1955), 27, 60, 63

Buber, Martin on adversity, 19

Buddhism: affinities with stoicism, ix, 7–9, 38; on judging others, 34; on staying in the moment, 43; teachings